Holy Doubt

HOPE FOR FRACTURED FAITH AND QUESTIONING HEARTS

Erica Barthalow

Publisher's Note: Events and conversations have been reconstructed from the author's memory, fallible as it may be.

All Scripture quotations are taken from *The Message,* copyright © 1993, 1994, 1995, 1996, 2000, 2001, 2002 by Eugene H Peterson. Used by permission of NavPress. All rights reserved. Represented by Tyndale House Publishers, Inc.

Book Layout ©2017 BookDesignTemplates.com

Cover design by nevergohungry
Author photo by Joy Mummelthei

Holy Doubt/ Erica Barthalow. —2nd ed.
ISBN 978-0-9989953-2-8

Contents

To God, who writes the most beautiful stories in breath and words, flesh and bone. I'm eternally grateful for the story you're writing through me. Without you, I have no story to tell.

To Jonathan, Jacob, and Juliana, for giving me a reason to step away from the edge.

To India, for being the most difficult and magnificent place I've ever called home, and for teaching me what it means to find my strength in God.

Thank You!

By purchasing this book, you're helping women around the world break the cycle of poverty and provide a brighter future for their families and the communities in which they live. A portion of the net proceeds from the sale of this book will be given to Convoy of Hope's Women's Empowerment Initiative. Convoy does important work in countries around the world to educate and train women in the developing world, giving them the skills necessary to earn an income and support their families, restoring hope and dignity where it's sometimes been lacking. To learn more and hear the stories of women whose lives have been changed by this incredible ministry you can check them out online: www.convoyofhope.org/what-we-do/womens-empowerment/

Foreword

Put your seatbelt on. You are in for a ride that is likely to rock your world. Perhaps you have questions about God and His goodness. You may even find yourself disillusioned and disappointed. If so, it is no accident that you picked up this book. God will speak to you through Erica Barthalow's personal journey.

It is no accident that you picked up this book.

Others have had similar experiences, but few others have been so open with their pain and doubt. Erica helps us see that every event in life works for our good. Though some circumstances are our own doing, God is right in the middle of it all—pursuing, gently guiding, whispering encouragement and calling us to a new level of intimacy with Him.

Though some questions will never be answered this side of heaven, Erica reminds us that God is inherently good. He doesn't always do things our way, but we can trust Him to guard our back and guide us in the right direction.

Holy Doubt puts our doubts in perspective. Despite our questions and hardships, Erica helps us peer above life's obstacles and find greater joy and peace.

Your story probably looks different than Erica's. But you will likely find yourself in these pages.

May you look back on this book and say it helped you go to a new level of honesty, authenticity and trust. And as a result, Jesus has never felt closer.

Doree and Hal Donaldson
Founders of Convoy of Hope

Part I: Is God Good?

Those who believe they believe in God, but without passion in the heart, without anguish of mind, without uncertainty, without doubt, and even at times without despair, believe only in the idea of God, and not in God himself.

—UNAMUNO

Introduction

Once upon a time my life was *not* a fairy tale. Pretty far from it actually, and if you picked this book off the shelf I'm guessing maybe yours isn't either. Let's be honest; Life isn't a fairy tale. Neither is faith. The tragedies of life can leave us shaking our fists in the air asking, "Where are you, God? Are you asleep? Do you see what's happening down here?" and wondering if he's even listening.

If you're reading this book, there's a high probability that religion and God might be dirty words for you right now. Stirring up feelings of pain, hurt, and rejection.

If that's true, it's quite likely that maybe you and God, and by default you and the church, were at one time on good terms, but right now you're on the outs. For any number of reasons the relationship is broken and you feel burned by religion, the church, church people, God, or any combination thereof. You're discouraged and disillusioned because your faith didn't turn out the way you thought it should, or you feel like God, or the church, let you down in some way.

I get it.

This book was written for you—to you.

Because I know how that feels.

In 2007, I found myself in exactly that spot, at a devastating crossroads between what I had been taught about God my entire life and what I was actually experiencing on a day to day basis. I was living in India as a missionary when my faith completely unraveled.

Awkward.

And a pretty big problem, because most of what I would've said about God during that time would not have been approved by our missions organization.

Some of what's contained in these pages is extremely practical bits that emerged from a season in my life where I didn't feel like God was trustworthy. Much of it is intensely personal, with the hope that my doubts, questions, and experiences will be of solace to you in your own struggles with God. You are not alone.

In her book *Walking on Water*, Madeline L'Engle says, "Generally what is more important than getting watertight answers is learning to ask the right questions."[1] I couldn't agree more. Questions are powerful beyond measure, and they do not intimidate God.

So dive deep, my friend. You never know where an honest question will lead you.

To that end, each section of *Holy Doubt* begins with a question that I needed to confront with honesty and wrestle through. It's then illustrated by a snapshot from my life in India and the way those experiences influenced my view of God.

While the book is organized into what appears to be some sense of order this was not a linear process. Oh, no. Quite the opposite. I didn't move through one question per month, checking it off an imaginary list like a manic overachiever. There was a lot of overlapping and circling back to the same questions as they popped up over and over again. This story was drawn out over months and years and, quite frankly, I didn't even recognize or realize the way my faith was changing at the time.

As I read books about God during my crisis of faith, I sometimes wanted to throw them across the room and scream, "You don't understand my life!" Bold promises to give me answers to my deepest questions about God failed to deliver because they didn't start where I was. Jumping right in with a 200-page exposition on the goodness of God left me cold because I just wasn't there yet. It felt like they skipped over volumes and volumes of grit and pain—the hard stuff, the stuff I was actually feeling—and went straight for the canned, easy stuff I just couldn't swallow anymore.

More than anything I longed for the author to stop being a professor, droning on about what I should think and believe, and just be a human being, someone who could relate to my questions and uncertainty. I wanted common ground, a point of connection. I wanted to know they understood what it felt like to be at the bottom of a black hole of doubt wondering if they'd ever see daylight again, and from there show me the way out.

I wanted to know they understood what it felt like to be at the bottom of a black hole of doubt wondering if they'd ever see daylight again, and from there show me the way out.

Reading those books was like listening to a friend tell me about Mark—a really nice guy who volunteers at the humane society and never talks on his cell phone in the checkout line. But then I meet Mark for myself and he actually seems like a huge jerk. I rush back to my friend to tell her what I saw: "He punted a cat off the sidewalk, literally drop-kicked it into outer space, and then stole a cup of coffee right out of the hands of an old lady at the bus stop."

Clearly my experience with Mark doesn't match her description, and this is her chance to explain his behavior. But instead of explaining the situation—that he was just kicking a really realistic looking stuffed animal back to some kids at the park and saving the old lady from scalding herself on a piping hot cup of joe—she just keeps telling me how great he is. Eventually, I start to tune her out and think she's delusional, or at the very least that we have extremely different definitions of the phrase "nice guy."

Unfortunately, that was the case for some of the books I read. They extolled all the virtues of God and forgot to address my experiences that seemed incongruent.

Maybe you've built your entire life—your very foundation—on God, and now that base feels faulty and crumbly, like the earth is opening up under your feet and threatening to swallow you whole. I certainly remember what that feels like.

When my faith started to display the fissures of doubt, I didn't know if I was going to make it back to God. He seemed like a dangerous and volatile place to put my trust. I wasn't sure where (or if) I'd be standing when the earth finally quieted beneath my feet. Or if I even cared anymore. I just wanted the shaking to stop for five minutes.

This is the story of what my faith looked like when the dust settled.

If you can relate, if you're feeling unsettled and uncertain, you're in the right place. Come with me to India. The place where I lost my religion—but found Jesus.

CHAPTER ONE

Abandoned

Northern India—October 2007

Inching my toes closer and closer to the edge of the steep cliff, I peered down the mountainside. The valley floor was obscured by ancient trees reaching evergreen branches toward me. Imagining myself tumbling down the side, I wondered if I would feel the punishing blows of each tree on my way down or if I would pass out before I hit the bottom. Numb. No longer caught in the suffocating grasp of anxiety or my own self-loathing, unable to feel any of that ever again. How I ached to feel nothing.

As I stood there contemplating how it would feel to step off that edge, a thought flitted through my mind. *I wonder if they'll ever find my body? Will my family think I just disappeared? That I left them?* I sucked in my breath and stepped back, crushed to think they might believe I'd abandoned them. I never wanted my kids to know the weight of that rejection, because I knew exactly how it felt to be abandoned.

First Days in India-July 2007

Just three short months earlier, days after our arrival to India as missionaries, four of us were sitting around on flimsy plastic lawn chairs in the near-empty living room of our friends' rented apartment in Gurgaon, a growing suburb of New Delhi. Scanning the room, I noticed mold blooming on the wall across from me causing the paint to flake into a pile of powdery white dust on the floor. My eyes nervously tracked back and forth as I watched my two toddlers race their Hot Wheels cars through it, leaving ashy crisscross tracks across the floor. My inner mother bear was roaring at me to get up and snatch them off the floor, pin them to my lap, and save them from a lifetime of lung disease.

As I watched them play and fought my instincts, my mind raced back to our second night in the country.

Our hotel room was dark and quiet except for the even breathing of my husband, Jonathan, and our two children, barely audible above the mechanical hum of the air conditioning unit that perched in the corner attempting a futile fight against the humidity of monsoon season in Northern India. We'd only been in the country for one full day, and already life was pressing in on me like the thick humidity. As I laid in the bed and stared at the gaping hole in the wall of the bathroom where mosquitos were swarming into our room I thought, *What have we done?*

A few hours earlier when we checked into the last available room in the last available guest house in the city, we opened the large wooden door to reveal what, upon first glance, appeared to be a nice clean place to lay our heads for a few days before we made the long trek to our new home in the foothills of the Himalayas.

However, after a closer look, I asked Jonathan with bewilderment, "Does it look like the covers are moving to you?" Stepping in for closer inspection, Jonathan looked back at me with a strange expression on his face, confirming my suspicions.

We would be sharing our bed with a colony of ants!

Dead ones, live ones, brown and black ones. It was like we'd entered a macabre Dr. Seuss story. I wanted to shut the door, get a cab, and head straight to another hotel. But we didn't have any other options. Turning my gaze back to the bed, I could see dead ants trapped in the cottony tomb of the pillowcases, and the live ones marching across the sheets and bed cover as if Napoleon were leading them into battle.

Jonathan promptly turned on his heel, stepped out the door to the front desk, and asked if they could rustle up new sheets for us. Nearly an hour later, we were still waiting and beginning to give up on the idea of fresh linens, when we were interrupted by a timid knock. A small man stood at the door holding a haplessly folded dingy sheet complete with dirty boot prints. It looked like it had been snatched right off the supply room floor, but it had one thing going for it--no ants!

Now that the excitement was over, and my entire family was sleeping peacefully, I slipped in my earbuds and locked my iPod on a continuous loop of Rita Springer's "Worth it All." While they slept that night, the lyrics: *It's gonna be worth it, gonna be worth it, it's gonna be worth it all, I believe this*, repeated in my ears, and I prayed. I prayed for the overwhelming needs of a country so vast and desperate that our family seemed insignificant. Little did I know, that night was only the first storm in what would become a tempest of fear and doubt that would grow until it threatened to destroy me.

"Erica, you're the calmest mom I've ever seen in India," my friend Chad said with a chuckle, snapping me back to the present and causing me to push pause on my trip down memory lane and my mental argument with my overprotective mom instincts. Re-engaging in the conversation about our upcoming trip to the Taj Mahal, I wanted to laugh out loud. If he only knew what I was thinking. Instead, I just stared at him.

"So Chad, what are your best tips for a trip to the Taj?" Jonathan asked. Having been to the iconic landmark dozens of times with various missions teams over the years, Chad had a wealth of advice to offer.

What we didn't know, and his advice could not have prepared us for, was that our first visit to the majestic tourist spot would spiral down into the "best left forgotten" annals of our family history. Memories of us sprinting the quarter mile from the Taj back to the bathrooms at the entrance of the shrine with my three-year-old son, Jacob, in dire need of the facilities—while an Indian family trailed us like bloodhounds, oblivious of our trajectory, begging to take our picture—haunt me to this day.

But I digress.

If Chad could have peeked inside my head that day he would have seen that I was actually a hot mess of anxiety and fear. I just hid it well. Not wanting anyone to see the worry beginning to creep into my mama's heart, sowing tiny seeds of anxiety and doubt, I put on a brave face.

> *Not wanting anyone to see the worry beginning to creep into my mama's heart, sowing tiny seeds of anxiety and doubt, I put on a brave face.*

From the moment we stepped off the plane as newly appointed missionaries, two toddlers in tow, we were ready to take on the world, armed with nothing but naive enthusiasm and sheltered faith. In the interview process to become missionaries we may have actually used the phrase, "start a revolution" to describe our unbridled excitement to share Jesus with the Indian people. All of the optimism and idealism you read in that sentence, oh yes, it's all there. All. Of. It. I remember thinking the expressions of the veteran missionaries who sat across the table from us seemed a bit amused. But no matter. We were going to turn India upside down.

Now here we were, only a few days into our mission, and I was already beginning to wonder if I had it backwards. *Was India going to turn me upside down?*

Because even though I put up a brave front, I didn't feel calm as my children slept with a colony of ants at the guesthouse, and I didn't feel calm as we raced to the bathroom at the Taj—finally being forced to take precious seconds to explain, "I'm sorry, we can't take a picture with you right now, our son has to use the restroom!" And I didn't feel calm sitting in the living room watching the kids play in moldy dust. I imagined them twenty years down the road, wheezing and wheeling around their own personal oxygen tanks courtesy of that dust.

Before we moved to India I was a laid back mom, unflappable and unruffled. But the overwhelming unfamiliarity of our surroundings was making me wonder if I had any idea what we had gotten ourselves into. I could already feel India erasing the old, familiar me, the me I recognized, and remaking me even then. And I wasn't sure I liked this new version.

CHAPTER TWO

The Unraveling

Northern India—August 2007

After our epic trip to the Taj, where my soaring expectations crashed and burned into a drastically different reality, we finally pulled up to our new home in the foothills of the Himalayan mountains and it seemed clear I should brace myself for some more mismatched expectations. Our friend, Tim, pulled onto the shoulder, put the car in park, and announced a little too cheerfully for my taste, "Here we are!"

I thought, *Huh? What do you mean, "Here we are?" What's here?* All evidence of civilization had been left miles behind us as we motored our way higher and higher into the clouds. Not that I had seen any of it, because my eyes were squeezed shut to keep myself from diving into the floorboard each time we passed a *lorry*, horn blaring and lights flashing, on the one-and-a-half-lane-wide-road with no guardrail. Remnants of past wreckage littering the valley floor confirmed I was right to worry.

As I opened my eyes I thought, *What is he talking about? Clearly, we're in the middle of nowhere.* I don't know exactly what I expected to find when we reached our new home, but this definitely wasn't it.

Looking out my window, all I saw to the left was the sheer mountain face the road was carved from, and on the right a dizzying drop-off with a spotty view through the clouds to the valley 8,000 feet below. The Indus River glinted in the distance like a silver necklace in the sunlight.

Craning my neck, the only building in the vicinity and in my line of sight was a square cement structure set just off the road, caked in a color best described as electric mint green. It had bars for a door and what appeared to be some sort of shrine nestled inside. That was obviously not our house (at least I hoped not).

Then I saw it.

A green tin roof sat protectively atop the gray stone two-story house tucked deep into the side of the mountain, mostly hidden by a thick canopy of trees and an overgrown cottage garden. As I walked to the edge and looked down at the trail leading to the house I thought, rather melodramatically, *So this is it. This is how it all ends. My children are going to die here.* Images of them carelessly playing too close to the edge and falling off in a tragic split second of inattention filled my mind. Shuddering, I turned away.

We carefully picked and slid our way down the slope toward the house dodging cow patties and trying to avoid the hulking form of a gray langur monkey stationed in one of the trees, branch bowing under the burden of his hefty frame. I felt a little like Hansel and

Gretel as they approached the witch's cottage, a bit of excitement mixed with a good amount of dread.

Walking up the cement steps to the small landing outside our second floor flat I thought, *Well, if we can survive the hike to get here, it's kind of cute.* Potted green plants sat in various intervals on the ledges, soaking up any solitary spurts of sunshine that might somehow sneak through the thick cloud cover.

At the front door a large rusty hinge that flipped down over a metal loop holding a padlock firmly in place greeted us. A small pinch of anxiety washed over me again. *Someone could lock us inside*, I thought, like any reasonable (or neurotically claustrophobic) person would. Popping the padlock open, we stepped into the narrow hallway and surveyed the entire place in nearly one glance. The house consisted of five rooms: a kitchen, two bedrooms, a bathroom, and a living/dining room.

Walking the short two steps into the living room, I saw a wooden desk in the far left corner next to a wall of windows, and above it a large, gaping hole in the plywood panel ceiling (an unwelcome portal to the wild outdoors yawning dangerously close to my bedroom door). I shivered thinking about all the creatures that could slink or slither through said hole and surprise me in the most unpleasant of ways. My mind was whirling and working overtime as I pictured myself trying to awkwardly karate chop a small monkey or a snake as it dangled from the ceiling.

Nevertheless, we settled in and tried to adjust to our new surroundings as quickly as possible. Since the process to become missionaries with our organization could best be compared to joining the CIA (there are batteries of tests and long interrogations...I mean interviews), we were in it for the long haul. We planned to spend the rest of our lives on the mission field.

Learning Hindi was the only real assignment we'd been given for our first three-year term, because being able to communicate would be the foundation for a lifetime of work. So signing up for classes was the first step in fulfilling our mission, but once again my expectations and reality clashed in unexpected ways.

I fully anticipated learning Hindi with relative ease. I pictured my passion and excitement bulldozing through any potential hiccups, but the daily struggle of making my mouth form sounds I'd never heard before, and finding time to study with two non-stop toddlers at my ankles proved to be far more difficult than I'd planned.

With each passing day, my mind a jumble of new words that just didn't compute, it became clear I wasn't bulldozing through anything. With that realization, my passion and excitement for being in India began to wane.

Growing up in Kansas, if I had a dollar for every time someone, thinking they were original and clever said, "You're not in Kansas anymore," I'd be richer than Bill and Melinda Gates (okay, that's probably an exaggeration, but you get the point). However, the truth of that quote became stunningly clear in our little mountain village. I most certainly was *not* in Kansas anymore.

Small, everyday tasks I took for granted back home became a process and an ordeal—one such task was washing the dishes.

Water was rationed and only "turned on" for a short window of time each day. During that small window, large reservoir drums outside of each house were filled by a central pipeline, and whatever water collected in our drum was used throughout the day. Needless to say, our habits were altered quickly because when the water was gone, it was gone, and we had no idea who to contact if we ran out (or if anything would even be done). The idea of conservation quickly became more than leaving a trendy note on our hotel room bed, to a matter of being able to get a shower that week. In other words, it was no longer an option we chose, it was a new reality to be accepted.

The concept of adaptation and conservation was new to our downstairs neighbors as well, fellow missionaries from South Korea who hadn't yet learned the secret of India: She doesn't bend to your will, you bend to hers. Choosing to remain rigid was an option, but not without consequence.

Coming from a country like America that preached the exact opposite, if you don't like something, change it, remake it to your liking and comfort, it was a hard pill to swallow.

Reframing your entire worldview is tough, a little like releasing a coddled domesticated animal into the wild and hoping it's not devoured by the first predator it meets. Our neighbors didn't immediately understand that even though they paid for electricity they still couldn't have every light and appliance running at once. We'd have no electricity—in the entire house!

In an effort to conform to my new reality, to bend rather than break, I bought two large plastic tubs for dishwashing and filled one with soap and water and the other with water and a capful of bleach. One for washing, one for rinsing.

One morning I walked into my tiny kitchen, which was no bigger than a rectangular litter box, to fill up the first tub and the water trickled out in a pitiful little stream. Soon the trickle slowed to a lazy drip and then vanished into nothing. "No, no, no, noooooooo!" I wailed, switching off the faucet, like it mattered. Nothing was coming out anyway.

Nor would it for three whole weeks.

The next twenty-one days were defined by our family purchasing water bottles at the market, hauling them up the mountain, and trying to dole the precious liquid out in such a way that we could wash our dishes, our faces, and our bodies, while still having some left for drinking and cooking. In a cement room off the kitchen, the washing machine mocked me as our piles of dirty clothes grew like an aggressive tumor in the middle of my living room.

Another necessity I took for granted B.I. (before India)—flushing the toilet—became a luxury as well. To say it was a rather fragrant three weeks would be like saying the surface of the sun is warm.

About a week into our stink-a-palooza my son Jacob looked at me and said, "Mommy, you smell good." Cupping his chubby little face in my hands, my heart swelling, I thought, Wow! It's a miracle! I haven't showered in over a week and my son thinks I smell good!

My pride was quickly shattered when he finished his thought, "You smell like a hot dog."

Our trial by drought finally ended when we realized that in the months our house had been vacant, someone had redirected the main water line away from our tank to fill a tank for a different house. The joy I felt when the water started flowing again, and the laundry piles started shrinking, can hardly be expressed in words. I would have broken into song like a scene straight out of *The Sound of Music* except for my new challenge—spiders.

Over the course of those waterless weeks I began noticing some rather large, unwelcome guests popping up in surprising places.

I'm convinced that spiders derive their scaring superpowers from their modus operandi—the stealthy sneak attack exacted upon their unwitting victims. Each night when Jonathan and I turned on the light in our bedroom eight legs attached to the most terrifying of forms greeted us on the wall above our bed.

Without fail.

Every. Night.

The spiders were about the size of Jonathan's palm, and when we took a picture of one it had red-eye—actual red-eye! I took this as definitive proof of their evil nature. Fortunately, they weren't poisonous, and even though I've always been afraid of spiders, I started to get used to them. Yes, I got used to the monstrous, tarantula-like spiders that managed to be everywhere I looked, all the time. Soon, they became part of the "character" of the house, and I barely jumped the day I was sitting on the toilet and saw one sprawled across the shower curtain inches from my arm.

Up to this point, everything I experienced was so brand new that I took our living conditions and house "guests" in stride, thinking of it as an adventure. But with each passing day, and each new surprise, the sense of adventure was starting to wear thin.

The life of a missionary was supposed to be glamorous and sexy; living in exotic locations, people coming to know Jesus by the thousands. Those were the highlight reels I was exposed to as a girl growing up in church. But that was not my life. Not even close.

The level of humidity in our little mountain village meant I got up every morning to moss growing on my shoes, and hair that looked like I stuck a fork in an electrical socket. Then I hiked my way to language school to awkwardly pronounce words that didn't sit well on my tongue, finally returning "home" in the afternoon to ward off spiders and scorpions from my children's room.

Every day.

Certainly nothing to write home about or shout from the mountaintops. There were no highlight reels here, folks. Just cold, hard reality, in a dose I was completely unprepared for.

> *There were no highlight reels here, folks. Just cold, hard reality, in a dose I was completely unprepared for.*

Since nothing I was experiencing had ever been shared by missionaries who spoke at my church (probably because no one but close family and friends want to hear about the hard, everyday stuff) I assumed I must be a failure.

Why didn't I have incredible victories to report and a bright shiny sense of purpose propelling me out of bed each day? I'd always believed that missionaries were somehow immune to common human emotions like fear and doubt. Well, I must have been absent the day God handed out the superhuman, super-spiritual shots to all of the missionaries, because I was feeling far too human for my liking.

My next surprise sucked any remaining sense of adventure—and any illusions I may have had about superhuman spirituality—out of me completely.

The front door of our house had a gap nearly a foot tall between the threshold and the bottom of the door, allowing any small animal or reptile unrestricted access to our home. I hadn't devoted much brainpower to that possibility until I walked into the kitchen one morning and found tiny prints in the flour dust on my black stone countertop. Heart frozen, I screamed for Jonathan.

He made a trip that day (probably within the next five minutes) down to *Sadarji's* store to buy some rodent traps. He settled on a model that was about the length of my forearm and had humane holes for whatever vile creature it contained to continue its wretched existence (how thoughtful of the trap designers).

Not sure what we would catch, I was hopeful it was just an itty-bitty mouse. But I was painfully aware that my children's bedroom was just a step away from the kitchen, and whatever rodent was feasting on the bounty in my kitchen could very easily (and quickly) reach my children each night as they lay defenseless, sleeping.

Looking back, I can see that was the dark moment when the root of anxiety first staked its claim over my mind. I can still feel the tight knot of fear building in my belly as everything within me wanted to protect my kids from these dangerous, disease-ridden animals, but with each new "catch" feeling powerless to do so. I couldn't understand why God would bring us to a place where I couldn't protect my children. Where every moment was an all-consuming struggle just to make sure they were safe.

> *That was the dark moment when the root of anxiety first staked its claim over my mind.*

The rats caught from our kitchen filled the entire trap (the length of my forearm, may I remind you). They were the size of a small cat. Notice I said rats—with an "s." We bought more traps, and in the end I'm not sure how many there were. I'm confident Jonathan tried to hide that information from me.

Late night, or all-night, vigils outside of Jacob and Juliana's room became my norm as nearly every waking thought was consumed by the rabies or plague-infested rodents that I knew lurked in tucked away corners of my home, waiting for me to go to bed so they'd have the run of the place. It might sound crazy, but I imagined them climbing onto my children as they slept and sinking their disgusting teeth into Jacob and Juliana's little arms or faces. Most nights I sat up until the wee hours of the morning and my eyes needed to be propped open with toothpicks. Then I would wander to my own spider-ridden bedroom and collapse into bed.

But the rats haunted me even there.

Scritch, scritch, scraaaatch.

Rat claws scratching the wooden ceiling above our bed was my soundtrack while I attempted to sleep. Lying awake, paralyzed with terror, I waited for the night when they would finally scratch a hole straight through the thin plywood sheet separating us and their furry bodies and sharp claws would drop onto my face. *Scritch, scriiitttchhhh, scritch.*

Helpless, I laid there waiting for my nightmare to come true.

A few days earlier my friend, Jaylyn, told me a story that shook me to my core and left me wondering if we'd even make it out of India alive.

We were sitting in a sunny cafe, chatting over some steaming cups of chai, when we heard screaming in the kitchen and the clatter of pans hitting the concrete floor. Popping out of our chairs, we came face to face with a giant *bunder* monkey clutching a loaf of freshly baked bread in his hands, frantically searching for a speedy exit from the scene of his crime.

After crashing through the cafe for a few minutes, knocking over tables and chairs like a barroom brawler, he finally found an open window and proceeded to sit on the balcony and eat the bread in plain sight, taunting us with each bite.

Glaring at the monkey, we sat back down and waited for the blood to stop pounding in our ears. But what Jaylyn said next did nothing to help me relax.

"Meheshuri went to the hospital yesterday," she said.

Meheshuri was the Indian woman who helped Jaylyn clean her home and had become like a member of her family.

"What? Why?" I asked, assuming she probably had a stomach bug or some other common ailment.

"Well, last night while she was sleeping she thought her husband was kissing her face, but," she paused as if reluctant to go on, "when she woke up she realized it was a rat."

No. Words.

Meheshuri had lived my nightmare. Any trace of the idea that I was being over-protective or ridiculous for thinking that rats could, and *would*, bite my children while they were sleeping was erased in that moment. I wasn't crazy! My nightmare actually happened.

I'd been fighting feelings of jealousy toward Jaylyn and her living situation; mainly that she lived in town, surrounded by concrete and people instead of the jungle and vermin. But this story only convinced me further that there wasn't a single safe place in the entire village. Jaylyn had just repeated my worst nightmare to me— word for word.

India was the first (and only) place I had ever lived where every terrifying thing my overactive imagination could dream up eventually happened. Monkeys attack a man and knock him off of his balcony, sending him hurtling to his death? Yep, saw it in the newspaper last week. Our water supply runs out and we have no idea when (or if) it will return? Sure enough, that happened too. Rats attack helpless, sleeping people causing them to need a painful series of rabies shots? Check, check and check. All of it (and more) happened. Daily. It was a never-ending litany of the stuff of my nightmares.

I lived in fear of the terrible scenarios that filled my mind and when and how they would materialize in our lives. *What kind of place have I brought my children to?* I wondered. "God, why did you send us here?" my daily mantra, muttered over and over to myself every time some new dreaded event occurred to remind me how little control I had over my everyday situations and the safety of my children. Every day I held my breath, waiting for tragedy to strike.

After Jaylyn's story, I was more convinced than ever of the importance of my night watches, even though I sensed I was coming unhinged from too many sleepless nights. My vigils stretched into weeks and then months of watching *Friends* reruns out of one bleary eye while the other watched the door to Jacob and Juliana's bedroom.

The longer it went on, the worse things got. My lack of sleep began seeping into every part of my life like a toxic poison, slowly corroding anything good and true. Including my thoughts about God.

So I did what any good missionary would do. I prayed. But God seemed painfully silent. The only reply I received was the unsettling sound of rat claws dragging across plywood.

> *So I did what any good missionary would do. I prayed. But God seemed painfully silent.*

In my day to day struggle to survive, to hold up under the new and unfamiliar weight of anxiety, God felt crushingly absent. And worse yet, uncaring.

Desperate, I cried out, "God, why won't you answer me? I'm dying here. I need to know you see this and you care." Nothing. Just silence.

I wondered what kind of God would ignore someone teetering on the edge of sanity, and the reply that came to my mind wasn't pretty.

All my thoughts were getting foggy, the only clear one, due to the constant reminders of my vermin infestation, was "Danger!" My mind was unraveling faster than the string on a kite caught in a tornado, and I was scared. Scared of myself and who I was becoming, and scared for Jacob and Juliana's safety.

Knowing I needed sleep, but unable to let down my guard, my mental state continued to spiral ever downward until the only thing I wanted to do was hide under my blankets and hope everything would magically change when I emerged.

But it never did.

Feeling like I always had to be "on"—my body existed in a constant state of fight-or-flight. Forget coffee or chai, my body was fueled by a non-stop supply of adrenaline.

When the stress of motherhood unnerved me in the States, I strapped both kids into his or her respective car seats and drove my mini-van to the Starbucks on the farthest side of town. That gave me about an hour of "off" time knowing they were safe and secure all buckled in, and if they cried I could just tune them out and be "alone" (all of the moms reading this know exactly what I mean). It was my mommy time.

Thinking maybe I needed some mommy time to help bring me back from my one-way trip to crazy town, I gathered up the kids and headed out in an effort to get a break. I quickly realized there would be no such relief for me.

The path from our house to the market was either straight up or straight down—there was no direct route accessible by car—and both options left me breathless. The former because of the immense amount of effort required to lug my postpartum body up it, and the latter because it involved a lot of sliding down questionable footholds and navigating switchbacks that were no wider than a cow, all while keeping track of two adventurous children under the age of four.

You may be wondering about my very specific knowledge of the width of the path. It was the result of frequent encounters with cows on our hikes and the sad realization that there would be no scooting around them. We'd have to turn around and go back the way we came, all our considerable efforts for naught.

The market was a riot of people, dogs, cows, monkeys, cars, trucks, taxis, vegetable carts, leering men, and motorcycles all vying for space on a narrow swath of pavement. Little concrete stalls with roll-up metal doors that closed each day like clockwork for an afternoon chai break grew like weeds out of the dust along the edges, small apartments stacked atop them like precarious Lego towers. Attempting to communicate with shop owners in my limited Hindi was often comical. Long forgotten Spanish words from a single class in eighth grade kept coming to mind as I searched for ways to tell them what I needed. I don't speak Spanish! And neither did they. Oftentimes, after an awkward game of charades, I just left empty-handed.

Visiting the market by myself was challenging. With the kids in tow the experience was unspeakable.

They were quickly swallowed up by aunties (the proper term for older Indian women) pinching their cheeks, fingernails poking their pudgy faces, as the kids wore varying expressions of confusion and fear.

I remembered another missionary telling me, "This village is the perfect place to avoid drawing unwanted attention for your fair skin because it's a tourist destination. They're used to having foreigners here." I won't say that was a lie—the village *was* a tourist destination. But it was a tourist destination for Indians trying to escape the oppressive heat of the plains.

So we were like a circus sideshow anytime we went out. Whenever we were in one place for very long, people swarmed around us like paparazzi at the Oscars, fingers and hands reaching to pinch, while their other hand reached for cell phones to snap covert pictures of the children and me that were used for goodness knows what.

On one of our trips to the market I ran into another mom from the States who'd also been in the village for a few months. Standing in the little textile stall, colorful fabric stuffed into every cranny around us, she gently nudged her daughter towards me and began rolling up the girl's sleeves. "I'm done with this place!" she pronounced, as I noticed the festering red welts covering the girl's arms and face. .

I could see that the pressure of helplessness had been boiling and bubbling in this mom since she arrived, and now she was exploding. All too familiar with that feeling myself, I could relate to the fear behind her anger. Completely.

Her voice climbed a few decibels and her face tightened with stress as she spat, "No one knows what it is! I can't find anybody who can help me!" Her final words to me as she wrapped a protective arm around her daughter and turned to walk out of the store were: "We're going home!" The finality of it made me jealous as I watched her walk away, wishing I too could get on a plane and fly away before my children ended up just like her little girl.

Over the next couple of days, as I thought about the mother and daughter in the market, anger began simmering inside of me too. I thought, That woman sacrificed a lot, out of obedience to God, to come to India, and it doesn't seem fair that God would let her daughter suffer like that. What kind of God would do that to her? I needed answers, and I wanted God to justify his actions, or inaction as the case may be. But again, all I got was silence.

Absence doesn't always make the heart grow fonder; sometimes it breeds suspicion. As the silence between me and God grew, so did my doubts.

Absence doesn't always make the heart grow fonder; sometimes it breeds suspicion.

Meanwhile, life was relentless. Most days felt like I was drowning in a wave pool, ten foot swells crashing over me, pulverizing my bones to dust. At best, it seemed like God was distant, and at worst, like I was an ant on the bottom of his shoe that he was actively trying to squash. I couldn't pray anymore. The words wouldn't form. It was like trying to sing with laryngitis. My mouth moved, but nothing came out.

My world went from big and wide open—tailor-made for moms with toddlers—to itty-bitty and hostile. I had moved from the foam play place inside Jordan Creek Mall in Des Moines that allowed my children to leap from the tallest point and land with nary a bruise or scratch, to a mountainside that if he or she did the same they would no longer be alive.

Our life felt small and dangerous. I felt caged and exhausted by the questions I had about God. Questions I thought I'd settled years ago, long before I ever came to India.

In the midst of all this—the anxiety, the questions—I was facing another challenge as well.

Vastly underestimating the effort it would take to survive in India, I somehow thought moving there would be a very minor disruption to the rhythm of our family's life. It'd be easy-peasy. I was wrong.

The exhaustion associated with raising tiny people, compounded by anxiety and sleep deprivation, left me feeling like a failure as a wife, a mom, and as a missionary. Most days I hardly wanted to get out of bed. All the passion and purpose I once felt had vanished. I had the productivity of a sloth in a coma. And coming from a culture that valued my existence by my level of production, I felt like a waste of space. So, upon my feelings of insecurity and fear I layered something new—worthlessness.

In case it wasn't obvious from the blind hope and optimism I entered India with, I'm sort of a Pollyanna. I always expect everything to turn out all right, and I'm woefully unprepared for anything to the contrary.

I'm not the mom with a bag full of supplies for every potential catastrophe. If you need a Band-Aid, I'm *not* your girl. I'm the mom who was drying her two-year-old daughter's jeans under the hand dryer in the airport bathroom before our thirteen hour non-stop flight from Newark to New Delhi, because she had a blowout and I didn't pack a change of clothes. *She won't need those*, I thought in my hopelessly delusional mind that always expects the best and never plans for the worst.

India was chasing Pollyanna into hiding and forcing me to ask the question, "What if everything doesn't turn out fine?" Because I was definitely not fine, and I didn't like it.

By now, our home instead of being a place of refuge, had become a constant source of anxiety, every day and night bringing real or imagined threats. I hated feeling trapped within its four walls, being at the mercy of all the creatures that also called it home, but venturing outside wasn't much better. Feeling like a prisoner, partly of my own making, both inside and outside of the house, anxiety was weaving itself into the fabric of my soul, holding me hostage until I felt helpless within its grip.

The higher my anxiety levels crept, and the lower my sense of purpose plummeted, the angrier I became with God. I didn't understand why he was allowing me to fall apart, why it seemed like he had brought us to this dangerous place and then abandoned us. Because everywhere I looked, I couldn't see any evidence of his presence.

In fact, everywhere I looked seemed to scream that he was absent. Scrawny, malnourished bodies by the thousands on the streets, rampant disease and sickness, unchecked corrupt systems that fed off the suffering of the people they were meant to serve. None of it added up, or seemed congruent with a good and present God.

> *None of it added up, or seemed congruent with a good and present God.*

Out of desperation, hoping there was some sort of solution we had overlooked, we sat down with a sweet lady named Saku who helped me clean our house. Jonathan and I sat at our table with her and tried to explain our rat problem in broken, halting Hindi. Her face lit up when she finally understood what we were trying to ask. Gesturing grandly toward the jungle outside our window she said, "Yes, one goes," her head bobbing from side to side as she spoke, "and more come."

I sighed, and laid my forehead on the table.

Only days earlier, as I sat at that very same table, I had experienced my first panic attack. Not knowing what it was, I just assumed I was dying.

Jonathan was over an hour away at the bottom of the mountain, and I was putting a puzzle together with Jacob and Juliana. I can still see the disjointed faces of

Jasmine, Aladdin, and the Genie staring back at me from the table, watching in mute silence as I stumbled away barely able to breathe, my heart pounding like the hooves of a thousand horses.

I'd finally reached a breaking point.

All the hope bled from my days, and I couldn't imagine living the rest of my life this way. Desperate to feel God's presence, I needed to know he was there, because I felt disoriented, unable to care for myself or my children, terrified, and very alone. I cried out to God with increased fervency, only to be answered by more silence. And when I read my Bible it almost seemed as if the words mocked me.

On one such occasion I opened my Bible to Hebrews 11. Wrapping my hands around a steaming mug of chai, I read:

> They saw it way off in the distance, waved their greeting, and accepted the fact that they were transients in the world. People who live this way make it plain that they are looking for their true home. If they were homesick for the old country, they could have gone back any time they wanted. But they were after a far better country than that—heaven country. You can see why God is so proud of them, and has a City waiting for them.

Those words sunk into my spirit like the bitter aftertaste of the water buffalo milk we'd been drinking. Throwing my Bible down, I could feel the weight of God's disappointment and displeasure settling on me, because all I wanted to do was go back to the "old country"—the States, the Promised Land. That was the final straw.

I was homesick and India was destroying me. I had moved there to serve God, to make him happy with me. I felt like this verse was confirming the disappointment and dissatisfaction that I was now convinced God felt towards me, since I was failing at my mission and couldn't even perform the simple tasks required to care for my family.

For my entire life, I was trained to go to the Bible when things were difficult or life didn't make sense. The Bible was always the answer, because that's where God speaks to us. But in that moment I felt like those words, the words that were supposed to bring me comfort, were slapping me in the face.

The events of the previous three months had formed a perfect cocktail of destruction, mentally and spiritually. That is what drove me to the edge of the mountain. When I stood there, the day after my son's fourth birthday, a day that, Surprise! didn't go as planned, thinking my family would be better off without me, all of my days stretched out before me in various shades of brown. Lifeless, dead, beyond hope. There was no color. No life. I couldn't see past the next moment, because in my mind the future held more of the same.

I've always hated movies about people adrift at sea. The monotony makes me crazy. I'd rather throw myself into shark-infested waters than drift aimlessly for days on end in a sun-scorched raft. Now I was living it. My life had become one long lost-at-sea movie, and I hated it more than those terrible movies. And I despised myself for hating it. The monotony was unbearable. And I was beginning to think maybe God was to blame.

Then I got angry.

Really angry.

Voices of people from my past echoed in my head, "God will never let you down. He'll always be there for you." But as I looked around at the burned-out, broken-down husk of my life, I concluded it must have all been lies. Because he didn't seem present, and I definitely felt let down.

If God was good, why was all of this happening? And where exactly was he? Slowly, I decided he must not actually be good and he certainly didn't care about me. In fact, I thought he might even hate me, because that was the only logical explanation I could extract from my circumstances.

> *If God was good, why was all of this happening? And where exactly was he?*

My husband calls the doctrine we grew up with during the 80's and 90's in our respective Pentecostal churches a "once saved, never saved" theology that pulled us to the altars every week like a magnet to confess our sins to an angry God. A deity that was just waiting to yank away his grace at the slightest failure or imperfection, and required everyone to dance around him on eggshells. Lord help you if you stepped too hard.

That theology left me with a belief in a try harder faith that could earn God's happiness and favor. I had sacrificed my sanity and our family's security and support systems to make God happy. What more did he want? Because he still didn't seem happy. Clearly, I had failed.

I had angered the eggshell God.

After two decades of serving God and trying harder, I just didn't have it in me anymore.

I was done with God.

CHAPTER THREE

The God of the Strawberry Patch

Is God good? It's a question that, after everything I'd experienced in only three months of living in India, I would have answered with a resounding "No!" Maybe with an expletive attached to the front, and I was too broken to search for a different answer. I had settled into an angry dissatisfaction with a God who had let me down. Big time.

Falling into a well of my own pain, I was surrounded on every side by more pain. The more twisted around myself I became the less I recognized who I was becoming, and the more I hated myself.

An overwhelming sense of failure stalked me like a ravenous tiger. Deeply hurting, I felt betrayed by my upbringing in church, but most of all by the God I had staked my life on and moved halfway around the world to serve. It seemed like a cruel joke to finally arrive in India and discover I was on my own.

In this season I was in no way looking for an answer to my destroyed trust in the goodness of God. In fact, I thought, *If he doesn't care about me, why should I waste my time caring about him?* Little did I know, I was about to hear a story that would call everything I'd decided about God, and his feelings about me, into question. I wasn't looking for him, but he was definitely looking for me.

Bangkok, Thailand—October 2007

I'd never felt so lost. Not in a churchy kind of way, but in a far more literal sense, like a small girl separated from her mom in the supermarket who doesn't know where to go, whom to trust, or how to find help.

When I finally confessed to Jonathan that I wasn't sure if I wanted to draw another breath, I'll never forget the look in his eyes. It was a soul squeezing mix of terror and sorrow. After a tearful conversation with our boss, we decided it would be best to get some distance and hopefully some perspective.

So we packed our bags and headed to Thailand, an oft-used place of respite for missionaries to India, and also the location of a counselor that some friends highly recommended.

"The first thing we're gonna do when we get there is make an appointment with a psychiatrist," Jonathan informed me. At that point, I didn't share the same sense of urgency because just leaving the village had been enough to lift my suicidal cloud. There was now color and variation back in my life.

I tried to protest—there were a million other things I would rather do than spend my time in a hospital meeting with a psychiatrist, and I had an appointment with a counselor in a few days—but it was futile.He was scared, and he wasn't taking no for an answer.

The following day I walked into the impersonal office of a doctor whose name I couldn't pronounce and sat down in the chair across from him. Barely looking up, he listened as I explained why I was there. Within ten minutes he had pronounced his diagnosis, quickly scribbled a prescription, handed it to me, and dismissed me from his office. Walking numbly from the room, I went straight to the bathroom, locked myself in a stall and let silent sobs shake my body.

Depression.

The word added another layer of confusion, shame, and frustration to all of the questions swirling in my head. *Why was God doing this to me?* Before moving to India I had never been depressed for a day in my life. Now medication was the only option available to help me feel normal again? I resented the diagnosis and the circumstances that caused it.

[Depression] added another layer of confusion, shame, and frustration to all of the questions swirling in my head.

Again I thought, *God can't be good. This is all his fault. I never would have been in India if it wasn't for him, and I never dealt with depression in America.*

———

While we were in Thailand, the missions organization we were a part of was hosting a women's event for all the missionary women serving in Southern Asia. That meant I was slated to spend the entire weekend with a room full of missionary ladies, all of whom I was sure couldn't possibly relate to how I was feeling. *Great. Just what I need,* I thought, as I tried to come up with excuses not to go.

With my new diagnosis perched like a cantankerous monkey on my back, I walked into the conference room where the event was taking place and settled into a seat, slinking down, imagining disapproving eyes drilling into the back of my skull. I'd never met many of the women who filled the room, and I felt completely out of place, both as a missionary, and at that moment, even being labeled a follower of Jesus.

Our host stood at the front of the room and said, "Ladies, I've asked Dalene to share her story with us today. She serves, along with her family, in Bangladesh."

She motioned to the side of the room where a woman with jet black hair that almost overwhelmed her slight frame stood from her seat and accepted the microphone. I don't remember much else from that weekend, but as Dalene started to speak my jaw hit the floor.

"I've really been struggling with God lately," she began as we all strained to hear her quiet voice even with the help of a microphone.

"My mom just passed away after a really long and painful illness, and I've been struggling to understand why God allowed her to suffer the way she did." Biting back emotion, she continued, "There were moments at her bedside when I couldn't stand to hear her screaming anymore, and I had to leave the room. She'd been a faithful servant of God for her entire life and it just didn't seem right." She shook her head at the memory.

I couldn't believe my ears.

Dalene's questions echoed my own. And even more amazing, looking around the room I noticed some of the other women were nodding and many had tears in their eyes. No one looked disgusted or even shocked that she was struggling with God. This was not what I expected at all. Was it possible these women knew exactly how I felt?

> *This was not what I expected at all. Was it possible these women knew exactly how I felt?*

Dalene continued, "One night, after months of questioning God and watching my mom suffer, I had a dream.

A huge shale wall stood in front of me, and I was on a small ledge with nowhere to go. I tried to climb the wall, but every time I made just a little progress I fell back down." Her hand fluttered to her side as she spoke.

"I got more and more frustrated every time I slid back down, and I began clawing at the wall, desperate to find a way off of the mountain. But the same thing kept happening over and over again. Dirt caked under my fingernails and hot tears stung my cheeks as I screamed in anger.

I finally gave up, slumping into a heap, my back pressed against the mountain face."

The entire room sat in rapt attention and empathetic silence, waiting to hear what happened next.

"As I sat there crying, I noticed something small and red out of the corner of my eye, just a few feet away, almost hidden in a cleft I hadn't noticed during my attempts to fight my way off the mountain. Through tears, I was finally able to distinguish that it was a beautiful, luscious patch of wild strawberries."

Strawberries were her favorite fruit (and mine too). Ironically, strawberries were the one fruit we were told never to eat in a third world country upon self-inflicted penalty of death from dysentery. Strawberries absorb the microbes and bacteria from the soil in which they're grown, making them strictly forbidden.

"I could hardly believe my eyes," she said, "and I wondered how or why a patch of strawberries was growing on the side of this awful mountain. I was so elated by the patch of my favorite fruit that I forgot all about the wall and inched my way along the ledge toward the berries.

Cautiously making my way towards them, I heard God whisper to me, 'Dalene, I'm the God of the strawberry patch—not the shale mountain. You've had your eyes fixed on this mountain for so long that you've missed this patch of strawberries I placed here to delight you because I know you love them, and I love you.'"

> *You've had your eyes fixed on this mountain for so long that you've missed this patch of strawberries I placed here to delight you because I know you love them, and I love you.*

I didn't hear anything else she said. Those words slammed into my heart like a sledgehammer, breaking open a small crack in the nearly impenetrable wall I had placed between me and God. Through that crack, a few questions slipped into my heart:

1. Did God and I have different definitions of the word "good?"
2. Why did hearing God described as the One who longs to delight me rather than frustrate me unsettle me so much?
3. What did it mean that joy and delight could be found in the midst of intense suffering?

None of the answers were clear, but I was thinking...

So, is God good?

I went through a large portion of my life believing, unequivocally, that yes, he was. Then life kicked me around for awhile and I decided he must not be.

But as I listened to Dalene tell her story, I knew I needed to know the truth. One way or the other. Because if God isn't good, if he isn't who he says he is, why would I want to serve him at all?

Part 2: Is There More?

The biggest human temptation is to settle for too little.

—THOMAS MERTON

CHAPTER FOUR

Pursued

First Days Off the Mountain—October 2007

Before going to Thailand, we were caught in Delhi for a couple of days trying to make flight arrangements, because when we left the mountain there was no time for plans. Less than 12 hours passed between the time I told Jonathan I was suicidal to the time we were in a taxi barreling down the mountainside, my head hanging out the back window because even carsickness wasn't going to slow us down. As we drove away that day, I didn't care if I ever saw that house or any of the stuff we'd left inside it ever again.

Some dear friends, Paul and Shelley, were kind enough to take us in when we got to the city. As we sat around their living room that night Shelley said, "Well, tomorrow is Sunday and I'm playing the piano at the international church. Do you guys want to come with us?"

I'm sure my face communicated what I really thought about that suggestion, but I didn't want to be rude. So I nodded, "Yeah, sure. Sounds good." Even though church was the last place I wanted to go.

The very last.

The next day I moved through my morning routine like an inchworm, hoping if I took too long and made everyone late they might leave me behind. I'm pretty sure Jonathan was on to my plan though, and he wasn't letting me out of his sight. Loading up in Paul and Shelley's Toyota Qualis, we crawled through Delhi traffic to the school where the church met.

Inside, the hallways were filled with clusters of expats talking and laughing. I watched them, silently wondering, *Why do they all look so happy? Don't they realize we're living in hell? And to top it all off, God has abandoned us in it?*

Incredulous, I walked past the groups of smiling people and slipped into one of the metal folding chairs inside the gym. Anger started to rise along with the color in my cheeks. *What am I doing here? Why did I bother coming?* I wondered as I watched the people around me sing and worship God.

Finally, the singing ended and the pastor stood to deliver his message. Mentally shooting down every point he made like a sharpshooter, I felt like every word he said was a lie. A lie I had believed my entire life. A lie I was done with. I didn't want to listen to someone talk about a God I wanted nothing to do with anymore.

God had rejected me. I rejected him.

The music started up again and the pastor said, "I'd like to invite everyone forward for Communion now." I was sitting on Jonathan's left, closest to the aisle, and he stood to go to the front, but I didn't move.

"Aren't you going to get Communion?" he asked, wearing an expression I'd never seen before. Shaking my head, I crossed my legs, forcing him to climb over me to reach the aisle and walk to the front alone.

Watching him from my seat, I silently seethed. I wasn't about to take Communion that day. Communion symbolized fellowship with Jesus, but fellowship implied presence. And I was convinced he'd abandoned me. So I wasn't interested.

> *Communion symbolized fellowship with Jesus, but fellowship implied presence. And I was convinced he'd abandoned me. So I wasn't interested.*

As Jonathan brushed past me on his way back to his seat I could tell he was upset. I wondered if he was afraid for my soul. Frankly, I was a little scared too. This was new territory for me. Moment by moment, I swung wildly between rage at God for leaving me and letting me down and the fear of being eternally damned.

Interrupting my thoughts, the pastor said almost as an afterthought, "One more thing, I have six copies of Philip Yancey's book *Disappointment with God* here at the front for whomever would like them. They're free. Please help yourself."

Jonathan turned and said, "I'm going to go grab one."

I thought, *Knock yourself out, hon. But you better hurry, before the stampede begins.* Rolling my eyes, I silently vowed I'd never read it.

As the pastor prayed a benediction, I almost laughed out loud. Just six copies of a book with that title? Who was he kidding? I was sure there were dozens of others in the room who were secretly feeling the same way I did. Their smiles were just a front to mask their true feelings, and I was sure he'd need a lot more than six copies to supply the demand. But there wouldn't be a shortage on my account. I wasn't going to pick up a copy. It would go unread anyway. Might as well leave it for another disillusioned soul in the room who might actually crack the cover.

As I sat with my arms crossed, Jonathan slipped to the front and grabbed one.

Little did I know, that copy was meant just for me. Had I known the role it would play in restoring my relationship with God I would have ran to the front that day and grabbed it myself.

Francis Thompson wrote a poem describing God as the "Hound of Heaven,"[1] relentlessly pursuing us with his love even as we reject and despise him. That morning I was unaware that the hot breath of that hound was on my neck, chasing me down, offering me that book, and unfurling the events of my life in such a way that I would begin to doubt my doubts.

The book was the very first breadcrumb in a long trail that would ultimately lead me back to God. And the questions that bubbled up from hearing Dalene's story a few days after getting Yancey's book made me a little bit curious...

CHAPTER FIVE

The Good Author

Bangkok, Thailand—After the Women's Retreat

Was there more? To God? To what I'd experienced? After listening to Dalene's story I wondered if I really understood God at all. Was it possible that I was missing something? Could there be more beneath the skin of my experiences? Unbeknownst to me, as these questions rolled around in my brain my circumstances were lining up to deliver some answers.

———

After being in Bangkok for over a week and getting a few solid nights of sleep, I was finally able to catch my breath and found myself looking forward to a long bubble bath in our hotel room. As the tub filled with luxurious bubbles, I searched the room for something to read.

Disappointment with God stared up at me from the desk.

Rolling my eyes I thought, *You've got to be kidding me. There has to be something else around here.* Anything else.

I scrounged around for a few more minutes, coming up empty. Not wanting the bathtub to overflow, I quickly grabbed it and headed to the bathroom.

Sinking into the warm water, my muscles relaxed but my mind was gearing up for battle. Even though I was pondering some fresh questions I was still really angry.

I came to the pages ready for a fight, prepared to pick apart every argument or defense the author threw my way. Knowing he was going to try and convince me not to be disappointed with God, I was ready with all my myriad reasons why that was never going to happen. From the very first page, irritation and defensiveness lurked in the not-so-subtle recesses of my mind.

For the first few chapters, as the book related stories of people who had experienced devastating losses and terrible diseases I felt a familiar sense of outrage and injustice welling up inside. *I knew it!* I thought. *This guy can't even come up with a good argument. Why am I wasting my time reading this?* As my anger reached a crescendo, I turned my attention away from the author and toward his subject, unleashing a mental tirade, a laundry list of all my complaints and betrayals. *God, you're just not fair. Why do you treat us this way and claim to love us?* The volume on my emotions was turned completely up, and I wasn't holding anything back.

Reading Philip Yancey's words that day unleashed a torrent, and my thoughts and feelings came pouring out unbidden, completely uncensored and unfiltered. It was like opening a too-full closet door, everything cascading out, never to be closed again because what spilled out just wouldn't fit back inside.

Some of the words I said shocked even me. I *shouldn't be saying this!* I thought. This isn't allowed. People can't say these things to God. I can't talk like this! I'll get struck by lightning, I worried. And I'm laying in a pool of water! I felt like the kid on the playground blurting out cuss words while all the other kids froze mid-stride and circled up to point and say, "Ummm, I'm telling!"

That was me, waiting for the teacher to come and wash my mouth out with soap. But I had nothing left to lose; I was already at the lowest point I'd ever been.

Coming clean that night in the tub felt good, a cleansing of the body and soul. Releasing the words I'd kept locked inside, that were poisoning my spirit, was cathartic. I wasn't fooling anyone. Everyone around me knew the contents of my heart and mind, (I've never been good at hiding my feelings or faking it) including God. Saying it out loud to him helped me admit it to myself, and doing that unlocked a level of honesty with God I'd never experienced before. To my surprise, I discovered I could tell God how I felt without being struck dead. Maybe he wasn't flabbergasted by my thoughts or questions after all.

> *To my surprise, I discovered I could tell God how I felt without being struck dead. Maybe he wasn't flabbergasted by my thoughts or questions after all.*

I'm a huge fan of questions. A good question unlocks my creativity and helps me see a problem from a completely different or fresh angle. But one three-letter question was chasing me around, stunting my perspective. *Why?*

Simon Sinek wrote a book called *Start With Why*, which as you can surmise from the title, exalts the virtues of that question. Ordinarily, I'm right there with him. It's one of my favorite questions. Asking it, shall we say, frequently, is one of my most endearing qualities. Just ask my husband. He likes to joke that if I found myself in a burning building I'd need to know why it was on fire before I'd run for safety.

When it comes to things like numbers, business, and organizational mission statements I think Sinek is on to something. Why is, indeed, an excellent place to begin. But when it comes to emotions, asking why is the kiss of death. It was leading me down a path of stale and over-tired scenarios, keeping me locked in a prison of self-pity and anger. I'm convinced that three-letter word has the power to destroy, because it almost destroyed me. That question is an insatiable beast.

I'm watching a sweet friend lose her husband, bit by bit. Will an answer to her whys ever tamp back the fear of facing a future without him? Will it return to them the months lost to scary questions and angry outbursts? Any answer to the question Why? will never be enough to fill up our empty spaces and erase the scars of pain and suffering.

Towards the end of *Disappointment with God*, Yancey writes, "The book of Job [in the Bible] gives no satisfying answers to the question 'Why?' Instead, it substitutes another question, 'To what end?'"[1] As I read that statement, I wondered if I'd been asking the wrong question.

I could keep beating my head against the wall asking *Why? Why? Why?* and reliving the same frustrating and traumatic experiences with the same dead-end results, turning myself into a bitter shrew. Or I could choose to ask a different question, one that might ascribe some meaning to those experiences. I could choose to ask, "To what end?"

God knew I needed to shift my focus, because I was on a path of myopic self-destruction asking why for the rest of my life. The things you keep your eyes on eventually have a way of warping your sight until it finally consumes your entire field of vision. A fresh perspective was needed. So God arranged for me to get that copy of *Disappointment with God.* Reading it, along with other challenging books were like eyeglasses for my soul allowing me to see him a little more clearly.

> *The things you keep your eyes on eventually have a way of warping your sight until it finally consumes your entire field of vision.*

Reading caused me to wonder and question even more deeply and begin to see my pain, and God's presence in it, from a new perspective. It helped me begin to decipher my experiences, to sort through my mess, and discover meaning. Because without meaning, I was hopeless.

And it helped me listen. Which was something I had stopped doing.

Reading the most thought-provoking questions, but never stopping to listen to the answers, or search them out for yourself, won't do much good. All you get is a brain full of complicated, jumbled up questions. Before *Disappointment with God*, that's exactly where I was, mixed up, jumbled up, and full of questions, but without answers or the inclination to listen for them.

I believe the best questions lead to the best conversations. I'll sit and talk for hours with someone who asks good questions and makes me think about a topic in a fresh way. But one of the foundational elements of a conversation is two people. Surprising, I know. That revelation was worth the price of this book (you're welcome). But somehow, in the midst of my pain and rage, I had forgotten that. I'd been having a one-sided conversation with God; furiously yelling, all the while keeping my fingers plugged in my ears like a stubborn two-year-old because I didn't like his reply.

After reading Hebrews 11, and feeling like the verses about not feeling homesick were slapping me in the face, I was resistant to the Bible. I wouldn't touch it, and I wanted nothing to do with it. Those words had kicked me when I was down, and I was wary of trying to read them again. But I did read books like *Disappointment with God* (a list of recommended reading can be found at the back of this book). Lots of them. And slowly, through their pages, I began to hear God whispering to me. And much to my surprise, he didn't sound judgmental or angry. He sounded compassionate and inviting.

Thinking God was silent all those months that I was spiraling out of control left me feeling abandoned and forsaken, which was more than I could bear. But the more I read, the more I saw God reaching out to me. Until one day I realized he hadn't been silent at all, I just didn't like what he was saying about me, and my circumstances, and his purpose in them.

Donald Miller, creator of StoryBrand and author of *Blue Like Jazz* says, "We're richly rewarded for listening."[2] As I started listening again, I began reaping some of those rewards.

Reading good books helped me process my emotions and give meaning to what I'd experienced. Their pages allowed me to confront some possible misconceptions I had about God on my own terms and in my own way. The books I read slipped past my defenses and helped chip away at the wall I had erected between me and God. They were a safe place for me when the Bible felt unsafe. Knowing others had felt (and said) the same things I did, but found a way forward, helped me re-open the lines of communication with God. Because I felt stuck.

> *Reading good books helped me process my emotions and give meaning to what I'd experienced...They were a safe place for me when the Bible felt unsafe.*

Sometimes when I'm writing I don't know how to get from point A to point B, and I'm like a hamster on a wheel, spinning round and round the same idea. Through the pages of those books, I realized God is never stuck. He knows all of the connections, all the plot points, and how to use them for my good. He's the ultimate author. He writes the best, most beautiful stories with human lives.

The picture of what God was doing in my life was coming into focus, but I couldn't quite make out the details yet. It was just beginning to take shape at the edges of my heart, but I still wasn't sure God could be trusted, that he wouldn't betray and abandon me again.

However, after months of reading other books, I decided it was time to return to the Bible.

When I opened the cover of my Bible again I saw things I'd never seen before. Through my pain-clouded vision, I only saw part of the story, the part that discouraged me and made me feel rejected. If I had read past Hebrews, in the very next book of the Bible, James, it says this:

> They put up with anything, went through everything, and never once quit (at one time I would've considered this a slap in the face) all the time honoring God ... (But I failed to keep reading.) You've heard, of course, of Job's staying power, and you know how God brought it all together for him at the end. *That's because God cares, cares right down to the last detail.* (5:10-11, emphasis and commentary added)

Had I read those words several months earlier I probably would have dismissed them, or thrown the book across the room. But as I read the whole passage and came to the last statement, I thought about the strawberries in Dalene's story and the books I'd been reading. *Does God care about the details?* I wondered. *Does he care about me?* I was beginning to think maybe he did, though I didn't particularly care for the way he showed it.

Earlier in James, he said:

> Consider it a sheer gift, friends, when tests and chal-
> lenges come at you from all sides. You know that un-
> der pressure, your faith-life is forced into the open
> and shows its true colors. So don't try to get out of
> anything prematurely. Let it do its work so you be-
> come mature and well-developed, not deficient in any
> way. (1:2-4)

Tests and challenges a gift? That James sounded like a real weirdo. The only people that like tests and challenges are American Ninja Warrior contestants. Not me.

But it got me thinking and asking myself if I had been looking at this whole experience, the unraveling of my faith, from a very limited perspective. What if there was more to it? What if the single most catastrophic season of my life was really a gift wrapped in some really ugly paper?

Part 3: Can God be Trusted?

As long as we know what it's about, then we can have the courage to go wherever we are asked to go, even if we fear that the road may take us through danger or pain.

—MADELINE L'ENGLE, *WALKING ON WATER*

CHAPTER SIX

Dangerous Prayers

Arrival to India—July 2007

It was hard to believe that only a few short months ago I was folded into an airplane seat, deep into our very first thirteen-hour flight from Newark to New Delhi, the legs of sleeping children sprawled across my lap, watching the small dot that represented our progress on the glowing screen in front of me make its way over Europe and the Middle East. We were giddy with excitement and headed for adventure. At least that's what I thought.

Before we came to India, I was living the dream: a happy marriage to my college sweetheart, adorable kids. Life was good. My biggest problem was having to drive twenty minutes to reach the nearest Starbucks.

Even though I had everything I ever thought I wanted, I wasn't satisfied. Something was missing. I felt like there had to be more to life than diapers, dinner, and church twice a week. And when I thought about my relationship with God, I wondered if that was all there was to it. It seemed a little shallow, superficial, and flat.

Sitting in the middle of my living room one afternoon, surrounded by stuffed animals and *Caillou* blaring on the TV, I prayed a dangerous prayer. "God, I feel like there has to be more to following you than this. I want to know you better."

> *God, I feel like there has to be more to following you than this. I want to know you better.*

Unbeknownst to me, India would be the answer to that prayer.

There we were, our dream to be missionaries realized, feet finally planted on Indian soil, stretching our sore muscles and hoping to get feeling back in the appendages that had fallen asleep on the interminable flight. I don't remember loving India right away, but it didn't send me screaming back to the ticket counter for a one-way ticket home as I'd heard it had done for others. Up for an adventure, this was going to be our biggest one yet—I could feel it.

The line through customs deposited us in baggage claim where we found ourselves staring at a huge "Incredible India!" mural stretching across the wall, complete with a large set of tiger eyes staring at me. I was captivated. It looked so exotic, and I couldn't wait to experience all of India for myself.

Quickly jerked back from my mental jungle safari (where I sat atop the leathery hide of a large pachyderm with pink flowers painted on its forehead) by two very alert toddlers bent on taking a ride on the conveyor belt,

I watched as Jonathan piled all eighteen of our suitcases onto several rickety carts.

Those black trunks represented our life, condensed into what we could carry (or more accurately, push on a dolly). Several of them were full of nothing but diapers and pull-ups. I needed an MIT math whiz to figure out how many diapers and pull-ups to pack for two little bums for several years. Not to mention what to pack for Jonathan and I to live for the next three years in a country I'd only seen in pictures.

The official-ness of post 9/11 airports unnerve me. In my humble opinion, there's no greater place of purgatory for a law-abiding citizen.

Where else is it perfectly legal and acceptable to have a complete stranger paw over every inch of your body and rifle through all of your belongings? Even though I've done nothing wrong, my hands get clammy and my throat feels like one of those fuzzy erasers teachers used once upon a time to erase real chalkboards, because my fate rests in the hands of customs agents who may or may not be having a good day. The power they possessed, to admit or deny our entrance into India, and thus our dreams, was terrifying to me. We could have made it this far only to be forced to turn around and go home. No pressure, right?

For a girl who frequently says the wrong thing (I have chronic foot-in-mouth disease), the airport is a truly terrifying place. For instance, the time I was traveling alone with the children and I thought the customs agent was making small talk with me and genuinely interested in my stay in India—as if she came to work every day to make a new best friend.

"How long have you been in the country?" she asked.

Thinking for a second, I replied, "Oh, about two years."

Dark eyes narrowing, she flipped through my passport as my heart fluttered like a patient in A-fib.

"I mean, I've been here for two years total," I stuttered. "Only six months on this stay. Look, I've got stamps from Africa, Thailand, Turkey..." I pointed them out, along with their dates as she turned the pages. Our visa only allowed us to stay in the country for 180 consecutive days, which meant we had to leave the country every six months. She wasn't chatting me up, she was doing her job! Imagine.

Watching her inspect our passports, I mentally kicked myself. *I should not be allowed to travel without Jonathan,* I thought. *This is a disaster!*

Finally, after what felt like an eternity, she passed them back to me and walked away without another word. Purgatory indeed.

Fortunately, our arrival to the country was nothing like that encounter. We breezed through customs and were finally making a break towards the exit, our trunks tottering like a JV cheer pyramid on the luggage carts. I held one hand on the pile, guiding Jonathan as he pushed the carts towards sweet freedom! Just ahead, the sliding glass doors beckoned us.

Out of the corner of my eye I caught movement. A guard in an official-looking olive uniform stepped into our path and stuck his hand out for our papers. *Probably military*, I thought, judging by the weapon slung over his shoulder.

At this point, adrenaline was fading and exhaustion from being awake for over twenty-four hours was starting to take over. The familiar feeling of airport dread crept over me. What did he want? I thought we were done with all the questions. Fortunately, Jonathan was there, because there's no telling what I might have said.

"Hmmmm, American," he declared handing our passports back to Jonathan.

"Why are you having so many bags?" he asked, gesturing to Mount Everest piled atop our luggage dolly.

"Do you have a wife? Children?" Jonathan smartly deflected.

The guard nodded.

"Then you are knowing why I have so many bags. The make-up, the clothes!" Jonathan joked, attempting to do a little male bonding. I half expected him to say, "Aye-yi-yi!"

Laughing, the guard said, "How long will you stay?"

Jonathan quipped, "That depends on how nicely we're treated."

Head bobbing side to side, acknowledging the wittiness of Jonathan's reply, the guard stepped aside and, with a wide sweep of his hand, welcomed us to India. We had to force ourselves not to run towards the exit.

Making our way to our friends' house that night I silently absorbed everything zipping by my window like scenes from the View-Master I played with as a child. Cows wandered through the streets eating from piles of garbage in the gutters. Tin shacks rubbed shoulders with shiny, modern malls. A cacophony of horns tooted, headlights flashed, and various vehicles and animals jockeyed for any open space on the road. Bodies huddled under thin blankets on the sidewalk.

Taking a deep breath, I realized this was wholly unlike anything I had ever experienced before. I closed my eyes and prayed. "God use us to make a difference in this country with overwhelming needs and poverty."

But God hadn't forgotten the simple prayer I prayed sitting in my living room over a year before, asking to know him more. He has plans for India, of course, but he also had plans for me.

CHAPTER SEVEN

The Gift

Chiang Mai, Thailand—November 2007

By the time I reached Chiang Mai, where I was to meet my counselor for the first time, my soul was as hard as a sunbaked brick. It only took three months for the adventure of India to wear off and my thoughts to be consumed by mere survival—and some days I didn't even care about that.

When Jeanne, my counselor, met us at the airport she walked straight up, locked eyes with me and said, "You must be Erica." Her gaze communicated both deep care and concern, and a confidence that I'd be okay. I don't know if my haunted eyes or my kids circling me like buzzards tipped her off that I needed that reassurance. Either way, I liked her instantly.

Stepping inside her house for the first time I almost wept. I hadn't seen anything so beautiful or tranquil in months. It was impossible to imagine any rats scampering through her bright, gorgeous kitchen. Her home looked like it had been ripped straight out of a Pottery

Barn catalog. She led us through the adjoining courtyard where an inviting set of patio furniture sat next to a soothing tiled fountain. I imagined myself sitting there the next morning just listening to the water gush and gurgle.

Opening the door to the meticulously appointed guest cottage she said, "Here's your room. If you need anything at all just let me know. Everything in the kitchen is fair game, and you're welcome to help yourself to anything at any time, including our library of movies and books."

Turning to leave, she said, "We'll go shopping in the morning to get some food that you all like. Get some rest, we'll talk in the morning." With that, she closed the door behind her, and Jonathan and I just stared at each other, speechless.

As soon as the door clicked, I ran straight for the shower, letting the hot water cascade over me for what felt like an hour as I cried hot tears of relief. Taking my time, I relished the feeling of being clean and warm—something I hadn't felt in months.

My showers in the village happened in a blink as I sponge-bathed from a bucket of water warmed on the stove, all the while struggling not to electrocute myself with the space heater that we perched on the sink to warm the room. The shower in the guesthouse, with its unlimited supply of hot water, was a luxurious experience.

As I laid my head on the pillow that night, for the first time in months not haunted by rats and spiders, I drifted off into a peaceful sleep. Something I'd almost forgotten was possible.

I had zero experience with a counselor, and I had no idea what to expect. So I was surprised when the first thing she suggested the next morning was not a therapy session, but shopping. Knowing I should get some snacks for my kids I quickly agreed, and I was more than a little curious about Thai grocery stores.

When I thought about counseling, I pictured myself sitting in a sterile office in uncomfortable chairs, much like what I'd experienced at the hospital in Bangkok, while the mental health professional tapped a pen on a legal pad and muttered, "Hmmmm," and "That's interesting," over and over in response to everything I said.

Nothing could have been further from the truth. I didn't know it at the time, but the ministry Jeanne works for has a core value of hospitality, and it's expressed by the counselor's home and life being opened to the world-weary worker—a philosophy that brought as much healing to me as her words. God knew this was exactly what I needed.

Driving to the market that day, Jeanne gently plied me for bits of my story. She couldn't have known, but asking questions while she focused on driving, instead of staring at me, was the best way she could have approached me. Having Jeanne stare at me as I cried would have been enough to make me lock up tighter than an oyster.

When I was a kid, I spent hours riding around with my grandpa in his pickup truck talking and laughing, sometimes singing silly made-up songs. I've always felt most connected, loved, and honest when I'm on a road trip. It's probably a by-product of all those hours with my grandpa. There's something about sitting side by side, instead of eyeball to eyeball, that unlocks the most honest part of a person's soul. Or maybe that's just me.

Pulling into a parking stall at the supermarket, we sat in silence as Jeanne processed what I'd said, and I tried to get myself together and let the tear stains dry on my shirt.

Finally she turned to me, green eyes sparkling, and said, "I think you've been given a gift." Pausing to let her words sink in she went on, "We just need to figure out how to unwrap it."

> *I think you've been given a gift...We just need to figure out how to unwrap it.*

I didn't know how to respond. Initially I thought, *This lady is bats! This isn't a gift! Did she hear anything I just said?* But on a much deeper level, I longed for the hope her words stirred. The possibility that there was something worth redeeming in all the turmoil and pain I had experienced was almost beyond comprehension. But she seemed completely convinced there was gold to be mined from the rubble of my life.

"I'm guessing at some point in your life you prayed to know God better?" she asked. My eyes widened in shock. Immediately, my mind flipped back to the short prayer I'd prayed in my living room in Iowa over a year before. Nodding my head, I wondered how in the world she could have possibly known that. "Well, he took you seriously," she said. "And this is your answer."

With those words hanging in the air, we got out of the car and went inside the grocery store, giving me time to process what she said as we roamed the aisles and returned to her house with the most delectable peach soda I've ever tasted.

Thinking about her words made me wonder, *Would I have prayed that prayer if I had known this would be my answer?* At that point, I had to admit I probably wouldn't have. If I had known the answer would be wrapped in pain, anxiety, and flat-out fear, I think I would have prayed, *Lord, I want to know you as much as a life with all my usual comforts, security, and stability will allow. Thank you very much.*

Growing up, I had a youth pastor who used to say, "I never pray for God to humble me, because then he will." His words were starting to make a whole lot of sense, because sometimes God's answers are a little (or a lot) more than we bargained for.

In his book *Deep and Wide,* Andy Stanley writes about a brainstorming session with his staff in which they were trying to develop the best way to help people along on their journey of spiritual development. This was the conclusion they reached about their own journeys: "As we shared our personal bouts with life's surprises and the effect those events had on our faith, we arrived at the following conclusion: It wasn't really the event itself that grew or eroded our faith; it was our interpretation of the event that determined which way we went. The conclusions we draw about God in the midst of our pivotal circumstances drive us toward or away from him."[1]

So far, my interpretation of the events and circumstances of the last few months were driving a wedge between me and God, but Jeanne was offering me a new interpretation. One I was unable to see for myself because I was blinded by pain and anger. But the hope she held out, open-handed, finally broke me.

The books I'd been reading were planting doubts about my doubts and softening my heart, but Jeanne's words sparked a new question. Could it be that God wasn't trying to destroy me, that he actually wanted us to know each other better? Was all of this pain and anxiety God's way of getting my attention?

For all of the stigma attached to counseling, for needing help to sort through wild and raw emotions, there is one great reason to do it—hope. Actually there are a lot of excellent reasons, but hope is quite possibly the most significant. I needed someone who could offer me more than pills and advice. I needed a lifeline, and that's what Jeanne offered me that day. All I had to do was reach out and grab it.

> *For all of the stigma attached to counseling, for needing help to sort through wild and raw emotions, there is one great reason to do it—hope.*

Often, when we realize we need a counselor we're at our lowest point, on a desperate hunt for help and healing. Discouragement, anxiety, and depression leave us vulnerable to deception, that's why it's so important to listen to the right voices: people who are hope-filled and able to offer light in the midst of darkness, not just a prescription pad and pill bottles. (Although if you need those things, there is no shame in admitting it. I did). I can't imagine where I might be today if I had never met Jeanne. My conversations with her completely changed my life and my relationship with God. That's the power of a gifted, faith-filled counselor.

So many people today go on quests to "find themselves." They embark on travels and spiritual rituals to uncover and unlock a part of themselves that is hidden from sight. It makes me laugh out loud to think anyone goes to India to "find themselves." The more Jeanne and I talked, the more I discovered I didn't like the person I found in India. She was selfish, self-centered, small-minded, and unloving. She also had some pretty messed up ideas about God and serious trust issues.

Before we knew it, Thanksgiving was upon us and Jeanne invited us to spend the holiday with her family, but Jonathan's cousins were planning to meet us in Bangkok. Putting counseling on pause, we flew to Bangkok for Thanksgiving with Dustin and Natalie and their kids, but I didn't feel very festive.

While we were there I found myself in church yet again. It seemed like I just couldn't stay away, as if there was some kind of gravitational force sucking me ever towards it. Truthfully, I was just desperate to be close to Jonathan. He was the one thing, in the middle of the chaos, that made me feel safe. Sometimes people drift apart when their world dissolves into madness, but we moved toward each other. While I didn't want to be at church, I wanted to be with my family. That morning, standing between expats from around the world singing worship songs I felt God ask me, *How's this working for you? Are you happier? More fulfilled without me?*

I had to admit I wasn't.

Actually, I was more unhappy and bone-tired than I'd ever felt before. As much as I believed life with God wasn't working, life without him was worse. I prayed, "God, I'm tired of trying to do this without you. It's too much and I'm exhausted. I don't want to do this alone anymore."

> *As much as I believed life with God wasn't working, life without him was worse.*

When we flew back to finish my counseling with Jeanne I had a completely different attitude. When she and I weren't talking, I was devouring the books she gave me, and I was more open to both the words in the books and the things we were talking about. Processing my experiences with her helped me unpack the questions that books like *Disappointment with God* stirred up in my heart.

During our time together I realized my faith was a hand-me-down faith; one I'd never bothered to make my own. It had turned to dust in my hands and ash in my mouth when it was tested in the flames of adversity, but Jeanne helped me construct something new, real, and wholly my own from the dust and ash. During our remaining time together, I was finally able to see a bit of beauty in the pain.

In compiling ideas for this book, I read this passage in Romans 5:3-5, and a lightbulb came on at last:

> And we rejoice in the hope of the glory of God. Not only so, but we also rejoice in our sufferings, because we know that suffering produces perseverance; perseverance, character; and character, hope. And hope does not disappoint us, because God has poured out his love.

When I prayed that naïve prayer in my living room, asking to know God better, I was really asking for character without the struggle. I wanted the end of Romans 5:5 without the steps that came before. The easy path. I thought I deserved the easy path. I didn't like the road this verse laid out, because suffering was the starting block, the foundation for all of the good things that came after, like tenacity and character. All things I wanted, to be sure, but minus the suffering please. I was finally beginning to realize that probably wasn't possible.

At the beginning of our time together, I thought Jeanne was crazy when she suggested that all the suffering and mental health problems I had faced were a gift. But the more I thought about it, and the barer and more stripped down my life became, the more freely I saw God move through it.

It became increasingly clear that God was asking me to let go of my comfort and perceived control and trust him with the same level of *dis*trust I had felt towards him before. But he wasn't asking me to lay that down without offering something in return.

One of the things I was discovering about God, that's consistent throughout Scripture, is that he always restores. He always offers hope. In exchange for giving up "control" over my life, God was offering me himself in a way I'd never experienced before. The gift hidden in my pain was his relentless pursuit and promise to draw near to my brokenness, to mend all of my holes and broken bits with his presence.

Had I known this was the answer to my prayer, I still wasn't sure I would have prayed it, but I knew now I wouldn't change it either.

I thought I could understand my anxiety and death spiral into uncertainty through my limited view from inside of it. I thought I understood the character and heart of God through my narrow, squinty eyes. Talking with Jeanne opened my eyes and my vision finally began to clear.

But what I was beginning to see was upsetting.

It turned out I was living my life, as a missionary no less, without God. I didn't need him for the brand of "Christianity" I was living.

In America, I could control my environment and my responses, and I had tricked myself into believing I had a relationship with Jesus. What I actually had was a little "g" god I had created to serve my own purposes. I served him because I liked the benefits, not because I really knew or loved him. India had exposed my phony, self-reliant religion, and God, in his overwhelming grace and mercy, was inviting me into something else.

Part 4: Who is Jesus? Really?

God is not what you imagine or what you think you understand. If you understand you have failed.

—SAINT AUGUSTINE

CHAPTER EIGHT

Fractured Mirror

Iowa—2006

During itineration, we traveled for eleven months and over 100,000 miles with a one and two-year-old in the backseat of a minivan. We met with hundreds of individuals, pastors, and churches to raise prayer and financial support for our time in India.

Our two-year-old son would stand on the platform of a different church every Sunday and recite his missionary kid (MK) pledge:

We're rough, we're tough, we've got the stuff.

We're young, we're bold, we're 'umpwetely' (completely) sold.

We're telling the story that must be told.

The task is great, the workers are few.

Turning his pudgy thumbs towards himself, he would say, "I'm going over. How 'bout you?"

The audible sound of checks ripping all across the sanctuary usually followed as people got behind us, sending us out to "tell the story that must be told" in Southern Asia.

During this whirlwind, we had the privilege of participating in several missions conventions at a few of the churches we visited. A missions convention is an annual event that some churches host which allows missionaries to share about the needs of the country they're going to and gives people in the church the chance to get to know the missionaries and their families.

At one such convention, I so enjoyed interacting with the people of the church, especially in the intimate context of their homes as we had "Meals with a Missionary" (opportunities for groups of people to converge on various host homes each evening of their week-long convention for a more informal, one-on-one experience with us). I'm convinced that many of the people we shared a meal with during that convention took our family into their hearts and prayed for us faithfully while we were serving in India.

This same convention was also a huge source of anxiety for me, because they had another tradition that did not bring me the same joy—or any joy at all really—the Ladies' Tea.

I would very nearly rather face a firing squad than speak in public. Maybe not even such a quick death, a slow, painful death would be preferable to standing at a podium with all eyes on me, waiting for me to tell them a gripping "story from the field" that will make them laugh, cry, and open up their purses and wallets to fund the mission. The problem was (1) I had to listen to several other women speak before me, and their stories were indeed touching and funny, and (2) I didn't have any stories from the field. We hadn't gone yet.

It's often taken for granted that missionaries are great public speakers, just as it's generally assumed that pediatricians enjoy working with children and veterinarians like animals. Seems to be a safe bet.

Not for me.

I disabused so many churches and pastors of that notion it's not even funny. You're welcome very much missionary ladies of Iowa who also abhor public speaking (I think it's a pretty small sisterhood, but I know you're out there).

I'm confident my public speaking skills became legendary (and not in the way one would hope). Once, standing in front of a mercifully small church on a Sunday night, I repeated, "Ummm, ummm" over and over like a car trying unsuccessfully to start while I tried to force a connection between my mouth and my brain. Fortunately, Jonathan recognized I was hurtling full speed into disaster and rescued me.

In a stroke of scheduling genius, the morning I was to speak at said Ladies' Tea we also had a meeting with a missions committee at a different church in order for them to decide whether or not they would support us.

Settling into one of the swively, padded office chairs that ringed the large conference table, my pits sweating and stomach flipping like pancakes on a hot griddle, I mentally rehearsed what I was going to say before the firing squad...I mean the Ladies' Tea.

This missions team meeting seemed like a perfunctory task to check off before I moved on to the main event

—the Tea. Well, I couldn't have been more wrong. A fact which became quite clear just a few sentences into the meeting.

About a dozen of us sat around the conference table, surrounded by bookshelves crammed with books, books I was absent-mindedly reading the spines of, trying to distract myself from my upcoming speech while Jonathan answered the committee's questions.

I was vaguely aware of the conversation happening around me, providing white noise for the thoughts pinging around inside my head, when suddenly the pastor looked Jonathan straight in the eyes and said, "We know you're going to make it, we're not so sure about your wife. We want to talk to her."

We know you're going to make it, we're not so sure about your wife.

Huh? Did he just say what I think he said? Surely not, I thought as I scrambled to re-engage with the room.

Snapping out of my half-listening fog in a hurry, I couldn't believe my ears. He basically told my husband to shut up. The room tilted and I felt off balance, mentally unprepared for the direction this meeting was headed. I felt like a balloon that had just been pricked with a needle, all of the air whooshed out of the room as I scanned twelve pairs of eyes, which were now completely focused on me.

Perfect.

"So Erica, what do your parents do for a living?" the pastor who shall remain nameless asked.

Unsure what any of this had to do with our missions assignment, but blissfully unaware of the direction the conversation was headed, I happily answered his question.

"Well, my mom works for the railroad and my dad is a contractor."

"Oh, so what kind of vehicles do they drive?"

"My mom drives a Mercedes and my dad has a truck that he uses for work."

"Hmmm, so that truck that he uses for work...is it dirty?"

This is no joke. I can't make this stuff up!

"Yeah, I guess it's pretty dirty." I replied, starting to wonder what in the world he was getting at.

I was about to get my answer.

"So, have *you* ever been dirty?"

Jonathan squirmed in the seat beside me, trying desperately to bite his tongue.

That's when the lightbulb went off. Realization spread through me like radiation after a nuclear bomb detonation. They think I'm a princess who's had everything she's ever wanted and never had to face any sort of adversity (or dirt, apparently) in my entire life.

They didn't think I had the grit necessary to survive in India. Interesting. And an unexpected start to my day, for sure.

If you thought it couldn't get any worse, you'd be wrong. The way things were going the Ladies' Tea was going to be the highlight of my day.

One woman (I wish I could describe what she looked like so you could picture the scene more clearly, but I've blocked it from my mind. I just picture her with a black pointy hat and a large wart on her face if that helps—just kidding, just kidding) piped up from the end of the table, "What will you do if one of your children gets sick or dies in India?"

First, what kind of question is that? Who asks that? Really? And second, right back 'atcha lady. What would you do? But seriously, it was at this point that I uttered a statement I would spend the next three years learning *not* to be true.

I took a breath and uttered these fateful words: "The safest place for me and my children to be is in the center of God's will." What I didn't know that day, and India would soon teach me, was that being in the center of God's will is not safe. Not. At. All. It's actually the complete opposite of safe. It's dangerous and difficult, and living in India would require more than I had to give.

Being in the center of God's will is not safe. Not. At. All.

Sitting in that room, I had no inkling of the many, many ways in which India would shatter my illusions of safety and hopes of living within a comfortable Jesus bubble.

CHAPTER NINE

The Testing

After Counseling–December 2007

A couple of questions were buzzing around my brain. Surprising, I know. Chief among them were: Did we misunderstand God when we thought he asked us to come to India? Was the timing wrong? Because I was sure that life and faith would be much easier if the kids were a little older. Did I miss it way back in Bible college, when I felt God calling me to missions? Because I'm sure it's now abundantly clear to you dear reader, I am no Mother Teresa.

Eventually, the real question behind all those other ones became clear, and the truth barreled into me like my dad's hunting dog, Rex, while I was waiting for the school bus in kindergarten.

As sure as I knew when my five-year-old body was sailing through the air Charlie Brown-style, that it was going to hurt when I landed head first on our concrete pad, I knew I was asking those questions because life was hard. Faith was hard. Literally *everything* was hard.

Even breathing, smog and pollution being what they were. But the real underlying assumption fueling my nagging doubts was this: If this life was hard, or met with resistance of any kind, then we must not be in God's will.

In the words of Andy Stanley, I was following a "Bible-told-me-so Jesus, and a somebody-told-me-so God."[1] No wonder my faith, at least the faith I'd grown up with, just didn't seem to fit anymore. Kind of like my raincoat that made me look like a T-Rex after I gained twenty pounds, because the fabric pulling across my back kept me from having full range of motion in my arms.

> *In the words of Andy Stanley, I was following a "Bible-told-me-so Jesus, and a somebody-told-me-so God."*

The often-repeated Christian platitudes, "God will never give you more than you can handle," or, "If he leads you to it, he'll lead you through it" (my fingers want to launch a full on violent revolt as I type those words) led me to believe that as a Christian I was promised safety, or at the very least, reality in reasonable doses.

Now that I knew differently, I had to go looking for the real Jesus. Not the fictitious one I had formed in my head, borrowed from others and cobbled together with scripture I may or may not have misinterpreted.

In the realm of strange confessions, I think this might top the list: I had never stopped to examine what I believed about God, or even notice my faulty assumptions about him. Seems like something I should have done *before* I moved to India as a missionary. But it suddenly made sense why I found myself in a crisis of faith when I thought I was following a God that promised me safety and it seemed like he led me straight into the mouth of hell.

No longer under the delusion that I was promised safety or experiences that fit neatly into the box labeled "things I can handle," it was time to do some hard work. It was time to find out who Jesus really is and build my faith upon that foundation rather than on my cocooned upbringing.

As it turns out, India was more than willing to teach me a thing or two. Handing me experience after experience that challenged every idea I'd built my faith around and molding it into the shape of the God the Bible actually reveals.

I'm not going to lie, I wanted to rush through the lessons, be "fixed," and move on. But God was unfolding a plan—one where my time with Jeanne was just the starting point in a very long journey.

One of our missionary friends would often say, "God is more interested in who you're becoming than what you're doing." At first, I didn't get it. And then when I finally understood it, I didn't really like it. Coming from a culture that values us for what we do, it's a frustrating concept. But it became increasingly clear that God was inviting me to slow down, to live in the pain, and learn the lessons that only deep hurt and helplessness can teach: absolute trust and sweet dependence.

God is more interested in who you're becoming than what you're doing.

The book of James tells us to count it all joy when we face trials and suffering because of what it produces in our lives. Up to that point, I had faced trials and suffering without joy, and the only thing I got out of it was misery. Maybe this James guy was on to something. At least following his advice offered some purpose in the midst of the pain. It may sound vaguely twisted and slightly crazy to say that the most painful season in my life was, without a doubt, the sweetest. But slowly, over time, it became the truth.

Our friend Chad liked to say that each time they returned to India after being away, India rolled out the welcome mat to a "welcome party from hell."

Had I known what I was walking into when we came back from counseling in Thailand I might have decided to go straight back to the U.S. But I would have forfeited one of the richest, and most challenging, experiences I've ever had. One that forever changed my relationship with God. It wasn't going to be easy, but I was finally looking for words other than "easy" and "convenient" as descriptors for my faith.

We were walking into one heck of a welcome party, one that would challenge every bit of the progress I'd made with Jeanne. The next few months were about to rip open fresh wounds and test my fledgling trust in God in ways I never imagined.

CHAPTER TEN

Brutal Trust

New Delhi–January 2008

Waking up that Sunday morning, I got ready for church completely unaware that my world was about to be rocked.

Jonathan and Chad were traveling to a remote village, which meant Chad's wife, Angela, and I were on our own with the kids. Fortunately, we were next-door neighbors, and she was gutsy enough to drive in the free-for-all of Indian traffic. So we loaded up her girls and my two kids, Jacob and Juliana, for church and prepared for the ride.

Riding in Delhi traffic with Angela as your chauffeur was like boarding a roller-coaster at Six Flags—you hopped in, buckled up, and prepared for the ride of your life.

On a previous trip to scope out a preschool for my son and her daughter, Mercy, we scraped down the side of a bicycle rickshaw while the driver, unexpectedly awakened from his nap by the sound of crunching metal, gaped at us from his seat.

On another occasion, deep in the bowels of our apartment complex, she was maneuvering the SUV through the tight, low-ceilinged parking garage when we heard a loud Pop! Like the backseat driver (and coward) that I am, I piped up, "Umm, I think that was the tire." Sure enough, we had backed over the spike strip.

Always an adventure.

But I was proud (and grateful) that she had nerves of steel to get out and drive in Indian traffic, because I sure didn't.

We made it to the guesthouse where church was being held that day without incident. Walking through the narrow breezeway, down the tiled stairs, we entered the room where about thirty people crowded together to worship.

Minutes after finding our seats, we realized the kids were going to be more of a distraction than usual so we marched our little entourage right back out to the small breakfast room that adjoined the church.

Tables with chairs piled precariously atop them, legs pointing to the sky, dotted the semi-dark room. The only light streaming in came from a couple of windows along the front wall. The kids immediately started racing around the obstacles, chasing each other and shrieking with delight.

Angela and I pulled down some chairs and settled in for a chat while we kept our eyes on the kids, reminding them to keep it down when their giggles got out of control.

Off to my left, I noticed my daughter, Juliana, had fallen down. Not thinking much of it, I turned my attention back to Angela. A few minutes later she fell again, the sound of flesh slapping tile stopped our conversation cold. This time I watched a little closer as she struggled to get up, flopping around like a fish out of water.

When she finally managed to get back on her feet, I noticed she was staggering around like she'd drank a bottle of whiskey, and one side of her body was limp like she'd had a stroke.

Blind panic set in.

The emotions I felt in that moment were unlike anything I'd ever known before. I felt like I was wiping out on a patch of black ice. Spinning around and around, completely out of control. I didn't know if everything vital would still be intact when the world stopped spinning.

> *I felt like I was wiping out on a patch of black ice. Spinning around and around, completely out of control.*

Noticing the color draining from my face, Angela followed my gaze. She stopped mid-sentence, and as one we rushed over to Juliana, now in a heap on the cold tile floor, as the other three kids gathered around.

"Kids, let's go!" we ordered in shaky voices. "Get in the car."

I scooped Juliana up and we all ran to the car.

On our way to the hospital, the only thing I wanted to do was call Jonathan, but he was unreachable in an isolated village. Thankful beyond words to at least have Angela, I tried to stay calm on the ride to the hospital.

Plunking down in the stiff waiting room chairs at the nearest hospital, I tried to breathe as I cradled Juliana on my lap. My heart was heavy as I watched the other three kids run and jump, skip and play, without a care, as I held Juliana and wondered if she would be able to do those things again. I silently told myself, *It's going to be okay. She's going to be okay.*

But I wasn't convinced.

When the nurse finally called us back to see the doctor he looked like he'd graduated from medical school yesterday; as we talked, I wondered if he'd graduated at all. In that moment, all I wanted was a doctor with gray hair and wise, experienced eyes. That was obviously not what I was getting.

"What seems to be the problem, Mrs. Barthalow?"

Setting Juliana on the floor, I watched her tip and toddle towards him as I pointed and said, "She's not walking right."

He watched for a few minutes as she bumbled around and fell repeatedly. Finally, he looked at me and said, "Well, perhaps she was not walking well before?" It was more of a question than a statement.

Angela and I looked at each other, exchanging a silent glance that said, "Is this guy for real?"

I bit my tongue and thought, I'm no doctor, but even I know children start walking around twelve months. Juliana is well over two years old. What was I going to do? Because it was obvious this was going nowhere.

After ordering a few rounds of tests, he sent us home with instructions to watch her and bring her back if she didn't improve. *There's no way I'm bringing her back here,* I thought, furious and scared to be leaving with no answers. I worried when, *or if,* she would get better, and if she didn't, how to find a doctor that could help us.

To my relief, her symptoms disappeared before the day was out, only to return inexplicably at random times over the next six months, stretching my new and growing trust in God in ways I couldn't have imagined.

In addition, a new problem popped up to keep me occupied in between her stroke-like episodes.

Diarrhea.

From the moment I got up in the early hours of the morning, until I fell into bed at night exhausted, I was bent over the toilet wiping tiny bums and going to and from doctor's appointments for *both* kids. I quickly became very familiar with every hospital within a fifteen mile radius of our apartment—to no avail.

Every test came back negative, and all the doctors assured us that Jacob and Juliana were fine. But I knew they weren't. Diarrhea for six months straight—all day, every day—is *not* fine.

Just a few weeks after my first trip to the emergency room with Juliana, I was forced to eat my words when we admitted her for dehydration at the very hospital I swore I'd never bring her back to.

At my wit's end, only treating symptoms and the doctors and nurses insisting there was no cause, we had exhausted every possible solution we could think of. I knew we couldn't go on like this. The longer the diarrhea continued, the more risks piled up, and the deeper I spiraled into a bottomless abyss of despair.

In the flurry of appointments and tests, I felt God whisper to me, "Do you trust me? With your kids?" I think everything leading up to that moment had proven that I did not. And this mess was just magnifying it.

Trying to ignore him, I hustled off to another appointment for yet another test. I was determined to find the answer to their sickness.

After still another fruitless doctor's appointment, I was forced to admit I didn't trust him. I wanted to discover a cause for the diarrhea and stroke-like symptoms so I could be sure to prevent it in the future. I wanted to give the kids a pill and magically make them better. Relying on God was hard when I stared into Jacob and Juliana's tired eyes day after day.

I didn't want to trust God.

I wanted a situation I could control, because I felt completely out of control. The same feelings of fear and helplessness that had stalked me in the mountain village had followed me here. I thought I'd left those feelings far behind, in my rat-infested house, but here they were again.

The circumstances were slightly different, but I was still mired in the same pattern of distrust and independence that made me spin out before.

As much as I disliked the situation we were in, it became clear God had a plan when I felt him ask me one day as I lay sprawled, exhausted across my bed, "Will you give up your perception of control and trust me?"

Did I trust him enough to let him do more than change my circumstances? Did I trust him enough to let him change *me?*

CHAPTER ELEVEN

The Monster Inside

In the beautiful and often ironic way God works, questions were part of my ruining and my restoration. God really must have quite the sense of humor. For the longest time, I was scared of my questions, scared of an essential part of myself, but God knew I'd spent way too many years with a "Bible-tells-me-so God." It was time to embrace the questions. It was time to be introduced to the real Jesus.

But before I could meet the real Jesus, he had to reveal the real me.

Counseling had exposed some dark areas in my heart, but there was more lurking under my carefully crafted Christian veneer. Before I could begin to better understand Jesus, he had to show me who I really was and why I needed him. He had already clearly revealed that I didn't trust him, but there was more. So much more.

New Delhi–2008

I slammed my car door, trying to get away from the woman standing on the curb in tattered rags, a squalling, red-faced baby on her hip. Sitting in the comfort of my car, the glass safely separating me from her, I studied the dirty bandage wrapped around the baby's hand. His wound, probably a burn, was full of puss and turning green.

Outside my window, the woman started tapping on the glass, gesturing toward the baby and shoveling imaginary rice to her lips in the universal sign for food.

Turning to my friend, overcome by cynicism and disgust I said, "I bet that's not even her baby. She's probably just using him because he looks pathetic, and she thinks she can squeeze a few extra rupees out of us by parading him around."

Equally appalled by the baby's condition, my friend agreed it was shameful, no matter whose baby it was, and we drove away leaving them both standing in our dust. We weren't playing her game.

I felt a small pang of guilt for being so callous, but I quickly doused it with a healthy dose of righteous indignation. How dare she treat a child that way!

On an almost daily basis, I was confronted with the worst human nature had to offer, and I was disgusted by it. It was unforgivable, the way she used that child to line someone's pocket with rupees. It was completely within the scope of possibility that he was mutilated on purpose just to play on our sympathies, and if we responded with a handout it would only perpetuate the abuse. He was a helpless pawn in a sick and exploitive system, but even so, something about my encounter with the woman kept nagging me.

The whole thing got under my skin and I played it over and over in my mind. I couldn't stop thinking about her and that baby.

The more I thought about it, the more it seemed like God was trying to tell me something. Finally, I sensed him say, "You're the same. You and her, you're the same."

The shock of that statement sank into my prideful, self-righteous heart. Outraged, I thought, *Please, God! I would never hurt a child! That's ridiculous! We're nothing alike.*

Twisting the knife a little deeper, he whispered, "That might be true, but you're arrogant and self-righteous, and more than that, you're blind to it. You and that lady aren't that different. You're both sinners, and I don't distinguish between your sins. To me, you're both the same."

God held a mirror up to my soul that day and what I saw wasn't pretty. Actually, it was monstrous. I'd always believed I was a "good" person. A good Christian. I was so good, in fact, that I had unconsciously tricked myself into believing I didn't need a Savior because I was so gosh darn good.

I'd always believed I was a "good" person. A good Christian.

Thinking about what God said, and how easily I turned away, unmoved by the suffering of another human being, whether they were scamming me or not, I realized I didn't know the first thing about love or being truly good.

And I never would without God.

At that moment, I realized I was so far from good that we weren't even in the same hemisphere. My pride and my own "goodness" were actually keeping me from God. In his mercy, God exposed the hidden truth in my heart so we could confront it together.

> *My pride and my own "goodness" were actually keeping me from God.*

It wasn't until I realized how twisted my heart really was that I truly appreciated the incredible love God offered to me. Love that was so clearly undeserved, but until that day I somehow believed I had earned by being such a good person. In a moment, all the illusions I had about myself and my righteousness were shattered.

I was humbled and broken, exactly the state I needed to be in to meet the real Jesus. As I let go of the god I had made to suit my own will and wants, I was amazed by who I found instead.

———

When I was a little girl I remember watching my dad wrestle and struggle with his faith for decades. It was obvious, even from a young child's limited perspective, that his doubts outweighed his certainty by a wide margin most days.

I can still hear my grandparents' worried and disappointed voices saying, "We need to pray for Kent. He's looking to other books for answers when the answers he's looking for can only be found in the Bible." The not-so-subtle implication in that statement was that since he had doubts and questions, (1) He wasn't a Christian and we needed to pray for his soul. And (2) that looking for answers to questions about God anywhere besides the Bible was frowned upon.

Those words, spoken so matter-of-factly, had a profound effect on my faith and shaped my beliefs about doubt and its place within my faith story in a subtle, but important, way.

Mercifully, India stepped in to push and scrape at me until my doubts became too big and painful to ignore. Forcing me to open the box marked: "Erica's deepest doubts and wonderings about God," that had been collecting dust in the darkest corner of my heart. It was time to walk those doubts out into the light of day and take a good hard look at them instead of pretending they didn't exist.

To my surprise, the deeper I sank into my questions, the more my doubts started to disappear. One would think the opposite would occur, but it didn't. The more I brought my questions honestly to God, the more I discovered his delight in revealing himself to me.

> *The deeper I sank into my questions, the more my doubts started to disappear.*

The God I was brought up believing in wasn't very compelling. How could he be if he buckled under the weight of my doubts? The God of my childhood was tame, predictable, safe and boring. But this Jesus I was meeting for the first time was the exact opposite of that. He was wild, untamed, and the very definition of love, and I was falling for him. Hard.

I had lived with a picture of God, not as a loving Father, but as a drill sergeant that expected me to perform, to measure up to an unwritten set of expectations, in order to gain his approval. My relationship with God was based on what I did for him, my love and devotion measured by my effort to please him. Try harder, work harder, earn his love. He was a taskmaster who wanted to "use me," and the moment I wasn't useful anymore, I was disposable.

As my life and mental state spiraled out of control, and I wasn't "useful" anymore, I was sure he would throw me away like a cheap piece of trash. But it was in that season of helplessness, where I felt I had nothing of value to offer God, that I realized I had him all wrong. He didn't want to use me, he just wanted me. My love. He wasn't a taskmaster, he was a Father who wanted a relationship with his daughter.

Hungry for more of this new love and his words, I started reading *The Message*, a different, more everyday paraphrase of the Bible. What I found was a giant chasm yawning between what I thought I'd read in the Bible growing up and what it actually said.

Amazed, I read story after story of people who suffered greatly and were still exactly in the center of God's will. Suffering was not the exception I had somehow believed it to be, and it didn't seem like punishment piled on people whom God hated.

Growing up, I skimmed the Bible regularly and familiarity caused me to ingest words but never digest them. I'd come across a verse and think, *Yep, read that before, a hundred times.* The result was a dangerous cocktail of knowledge with no real understanding or context to apply what it meant. But reading *The Message*, engaging with fresh words that often stopped me cold and left me thinking, *That's what that verse means?!*, brought into focus a whole different picture of what it means to follow God and love Jesus.

Basically, I was hooked.

Not on a God that someone else told me about, but the God I was finally getting to know for myself. The one he'd been waiting for me to see my entire life. Granted, it was a painful ride to get here, but well worth the price.

Some of you are probably thinking, "Well, that sounds nice, but why did God have to let you go through all of that? Wasn't there an easier way?"

I can't answer that question for you, but I know for me the answer is, probably not. I'm stubborn. It's part of what allowed me to stay in India for our whole term when it would have been much easier to just go home. But it's also the same quality that made me so hard to reach.

C.S. Lewis described pain as a megaphone through which God shouts to get our attention.[1] For me, God practically had to scream because I'm hard-headed and, as my son likes to remind me, hard of hearing. It took anxiety, depression, and scary illnesses for God to finally get my attention.

Now that he had it, it was time to address a misconception that had been hanging over my head since we arrived in India—really, for my entire life—the implications of which were at the root of my distrust towards God when my life rocketed out of control.

I thought serving God meant I'd be prosperous and safe, and life in India made it clear on a daily basis that we weren't promised another breath.

With not a hint of exaggeration, I can say in the throes of their illnesses I feared, almost daily, that my children might slip away from me. Nothing about our life felt safe, but I'd always believed if you were doing the Christian life right that you'd be blessed with safety and security.

Not that I was taught a prosperity gospel, it was just the only thing I'd ever observed in my little Midwestern corner of the world. All the Christians I knew were the very definition of safe and secure, and I didn't bother comparing my experience to the Bible. So when we moved to India and all hell broke loose, I thought we missed God's will, because God's will was for us to be safe. That was why I viewed all the trials and challenges we faced in India as punishment from an angry God. I believed we were being punished for somehow missing his plan.

One of the platitudes I heard growing up, which I believe was said with good intentions was, "God will never give you more than you can handle." India proved over and over, in a thousand unique ways, how *un*true that statement really was. Because each time I was given more than I could handle, I had to learn how to depend on God. Something I'd never really learned to do before. Oh, I thought I depended on God. I would have told you I did. But in reality, in my day to day life, I didn't need to depend on God because I could control and manage everything around me in a pretty pleasant way. In America, I trusted and depended on myself.

India changed all of that, deprogramming that ridiculous idea from my life completely. Looking back, the years I spent "in control," were the poorest of my life. Getting more than I could handle, being overwhelmed by my helplessness, was the greatest gift I ever received, because it forced me to lean on God. The more I did, the more I realized that was exactly where I wanted to be. Not because it was safe or I was promised a perfect outcome, but because I had a bird's-eye view to watch God work. And his work was spectacular.

As I moved from self-reliance to dependence, one thing became clear. I never wanted to live in that comfortable place where I had it all under my control again. I wanted to live at the intersection of: If God doesn't show up we'll be ruined, and I can't handle this on my own. I'm not trying to give you a romanticized picture here, it's just honest-to-goodness truth. If you set up residence there, you'll find it's both the scariest and most incredible place you've ever dared to live.

For me, what came of asking "Can God be trusted?" was an unshakeable trust in a sturdy Jesus, not the paper-thin one I had constructed from secondhand experiences. It came from watching him show up in small, easily overlooked ways to big, grandiose ways every day, at just the right moment.

It came from choosing to walk hand-in-hand with him when everything fell apart and I felt small and terrified. Philip Yancey sums it up perfectly, "Faith like Job's cannot be shaken because it is the result of having been shaken."[2]

India shook and shifted everything about me, from the way I pray, to the way I think, to the way I care about people. It moved my faith from theory to practice. When I was finally able to pray for his will to be done, for him to be glorified, and mean it. I finally understood that when I was so out of control, he was holding me in the midst of the chaos, and if he could make something beautiful and meaningful out of that mess, I knew I could trust him.

In Philippians, Paul talks about "fellowshipping in Christ's suffering." I'll admit it's a phrase I glossed over before. I never paused to truly understand or dissect it, but it took on a new significance to me during those long months that I struggled to care for sick kids and daily place them in God's hands.

On days when it seemed the bleakest, when our hours inside of the bathroom outnumbered the minutes we spent outside of it, he was close. I experienced him as the God who comes near. Who sits with us. It was a sweet time like I had never experienced before and honestly haven't since.

It was in the midst of, not in spite of, confusion, unanswered questions, and my children's worst sicknesses—which incidentally disappeared six months later just as mysteriously as they appeared—that I experienced a closeness, a fullness, a joy like I'd never known before. I *knew* that God was with me, holding me, my kids, and my husband close.

Looking back, I would never trade that experience. It changed everything for me. I would walk on burning coals for the love that overwhelmed me during that time. With the benefit of time, and the ability to reflect from outside the pain, I know I would never want to undo what we went through. Ever.

In the years since this book was first released, I've had readers write to me with heartbreaking stories. Often they ask, "If things hadn't turned out okay with your kids, would you still feel the same way? Would you still say that God is good?"

> *If things hadn't turned out okay with your kids, would you still feel the same way? Would you still say that God is good?*

I know those questions are coming from a place of immense pain and suffering, where it's a struggle every day to see any greater plan or purpose. All I can say, is that while I was mired in the middle of these difficult experiences sometimes it was hard to see his goodness and his plan. Sometimes it takes time, and a different perspective to see even a sliver of goodness.

Madeline L'Engle writes, "The unending paradox is that we do learn through pain...I look back at my mother's life and I see suffering deepening and strengthening it. In some people I have also seen it destroy. Pain is not always creative; received wrongly, it can lead to alcoholism and madness and suicide. Nevertheless, without it we do not grow."[3]

That quote captures the paradox of pain perfectly. It all comes down to this: Everyone has doubts and experiences pain. For a long time, inside my sheltered bubble, that was a well-kept secret. Not everyone doubts the same things, of course, but everyone doubts.

So, the question becomes: What do we do with those doubts? What do we do with questions about the character of God? Will we use them to learn more about God and our preconceived ideas about him, or will we allow them to destroy us?

Part 5: Am I Better Off Alone?

Walking with a friend in the dark is better than walking alone in the light.

—HELEN KELLER

CHAPTER TWELVE

The Ugly Everyday

India—2008

Excitement buzzed in our house. Our friend Dilip was in town and wanted to introduce us to his family. His cousin, his cousin's wife, his cousin's mother-in-law, and their baby were coming over for dinner. Essentially, my worst nightmare.

Before you can understand the gravity of my situation you must first understand something about Indian culture, and my place within it. In India, hospitality is an art form. Families who lived in two-room houses bought chicken and Coca-Cola they probably couldn't afford (and would never buy for themselves) to serve to us when we came to visit.

Jacob always said he loved going to the homes of our Indian friends because they gave him as much Coke as he wanted, usually over my weak protests. Our friends would just bob their heads from side to side and say, "Oh, sister. Let him have the Coke." How do you respond to such generosity and kindness? You don't say no, I'll tell you that. So I'd sit back, watch my son guzzle a liter of Coke and then ping off the walls like a pinball. It was humbling and sweet, and honestly, a lot to live up to.

At this point, almost two years into our term, I'd like to say I had kicked anxiety in the teeth and no longer needed the medication prescribed to me in Thailand, but I was still regularly taking Xanax in an attempt to take the edge off of life. But no amount of Xanax was going to get me through this day.

As an introvert, I enjoy being around people. But it does not energize me, instead it sucks the energy out of me quicker than an old cell phone battery can lose a charge. It depletes my emotional reserves, and my reserves had no excess to spare. For me, having people over to our house usually requires a mental pep talk and some time to prepare. Last-minute surprise guests usually guarantees disaster. This was never more true than during this season of my life.

That fateful day there was no margin to talk myself up. We had been out shopping for several hours when Jonathan suggested Dilip bring his family over for dinner, and I didn't feel like I could say no, probably because I wasn't given the opportunity to. Can you see the writing on the wall? It says D-I-S-A-S-T-E-R!

Riding home from the store, I immediately started mentally rummaging through the contents of my pantry, knowing they would be arriving in just a few hours for dinner. Nothing I came up with sounded acceptable.

Not only did I not have the right food, I knew I'd be a failure as a hostess. My idea of a great dinner party is food served buffet-style on paper plates so I don't have to do dishes afterwards, and everyone getting their own drinks.

Definitely not the Indian way.

To make matters worse, and further illustrate my ineptitude, I get lost in the moment during dinner and don't notice when people need more to drink. Jonathan usually gets up and offers to refill everyone's drinks. Double strike. Another cultural blunder. Each faux pas stacked up in my mind like dirty dishes, indicting me for the failure I knew I would be, and already was.

The more I thought about how deficient I was, and the more I remembered their hospitality when we were invited to their home, the tighter my chest started to feel.

Recognizing the cold fingers of anxiety slipping around my heart, sucking me into a familiar black hole, I picked up my phone and called Angela. Hearing the panic in my voice she said, "Don't worry! I'll be right over."

> *Recognizing the cold fingers of anxiety slipping around my heart, sucking me into a familiar black hole, I picked up my phone and called Angela.*

Hanging up the phone, I felt a little better for the split second between the phone call and their knock on our door.

Immediately, I panicked.

Jonathan opened the door, our guests filed in, and I turned around and scurried for the nearest hiding place, which happened to be my dark pantry. Standing there trying to get myself together, slowly breathing in and out, I listened to the activity in the next room, while shame whispered in my ear, "You're a failure, a real loser. Your husband must be so ashamed of you."

I slumped down to the floor, silently sobbing, as I listened to Angela effortlessly entertain my guests. *What's wrong with me? Why can't I get it together? Will I ever feel normal again?* I wondered. The sounds of my life played around me as I huddled in the other room hiding.

> *The sounds of my life played around me as I huddled in the other room hiding.*

I crouched there for what felt like hours, but was probably more like half an hour, until Angela found me. Sliding down next to me, she grabbed my hand.

"Why don't you go lay down?"

"I can't walk past everyone. They'll want to talk to me," I whispered. The thought made me wish I'd had the forethought to dig a secret tunnel from the pantry to my bedroom, in anticipation of just such a circumstance.

The problem was, I never saw this coming. It's the things we don't see coming that throw us for the biggest loops, isn't it? That's why we have doomsday preppers. They feel like they can face anything, a nuclear blast or the apocalypse, as long as they're prepared. Well, I wasn't prepared for this at all. Never had I struggled so much in social situations. I didn't even recognize myself anymore.

"I'll walk with you and make sure you don't get stopped," she promised.

———

That day Angela showed me what true friendship looks like, and how much I needed that kind of love in my life when everything around me was in shambles.

True friendship looks like love that forgets to be shocked when they find you in a heap on your pantry floor, and promises to stick by your side and shield you from the stares and questions of curious onlookers. It looks like showing up at your bedside, when your husband is half a world away and you're so sick with a kidney infection that you can barely drag yourself to the bathroom, to get medicine and watch your kids. It looks like patience when you stubbornly refuse to go to the hospital. It looks like two dear friends, dropping everything and basically moving in to take care of you and your kids until your husband returns. Hypothetically.

That's what friendship looks like. And that's the kind of friendships you'll need to help you navigate the convoluted path through doubt.

Whatever you do, please don't try to go it alone.

CHAPTER THIRTEEN

Community

Nothing good happens in isolation. I know this from experience. A friend of mine, struggling through the aftereffects of an unwanted divorce, had some well-meaning people suggest he might just need some time alone with his thoughts and feelings. Nodding his head he replied, "Yep, and just one bullet."

His statement bears witness to the fact that our pain aches to be wrapped in the presence of others. We want to know we're not alone and someone understands us, or at least empathizes. Without that connection and support, life is nearly unbearable, and sorting through our doubts and questions is so much harder. We were designed to share our joy—and our pain.

I can hear the arguments now. "But I'm an introvert! I like to be alone." Or, "I can't be real with them, they'll think I'm crazy."

I understand. I really do. All the fears and insecurities that go along with letting someone get close to you, especially when you're struggling with your faith, are overwhelming and terrifying. It's a whole different level of vulnerability and openness. Your fears are valid. But this one thing I know: You need people around you. Isolation is your enemy.

If I could have chosen just one word to describe my life at the darkest point, when I was considering suicide, it would have been: alone. I didn't feel like God was present, and I was hiding my true feelings from the people around me, convinced they could never understand how I felt. All of that isolation led to the death of hope. But it doesn't have to be that way.

———

There's a phenomenon that occurs, not just in dating relationships, but in friendship too. It's the "We could never be friends, because she's too..." fill in the blank with any adjective that supports your worst opinion of yourself. Maybe it's: she's too smart, or too pretty, or too spiritual, to want to be friends with me. It's the friendship equivalent of "they're out of my league."

When I first met Angela I was ticking reasons why we couldn't be friends off the list in my mind: She's way too perfect and busy to be friends with me, and she's way too spiritual to understand my doubts. I thought, *She's been in India for so long and been through so much* (I'd heard bits of her story) *She'll think I'm stupid for feeling this way. I'd feel ridiculous complaining about any of this knowing what she's been through.*

Planning to keep her at arm's length and not reveal my true feelings, I watched her from a safe distance and wondered if she was silently judging me. I'm laughing as

I write this now, because I know how utterly absurd that thought was, but it was very real to me at the time.

Somewhere between living with Chad and Angela and their two girls for three weeks while we searched for an apartment in Delhi after moving out of the mountains, and daily play dates with our kids, my defenses started to melt. Maybe it was her sense of humor or hilarious personality quirks, but when she told me about the time she lit her favorite baggy t-shirt on fire—while she was wearing it—cooking over her gas stove, all my reservations went out the window.

She was better than perfect, she was real. Charred t-shirt and all.

But comparison and assumptions almost kept me from one of the best friendships I've ever had, because comparison and assumptions are the enemies of true friendship. They're the lying voices that want to get you —and keep you—alone by whispering, "He would never want to be your friend. He's way too good to understand you. He's got it all together; you're a mess. You better not let him see the real you. Hide it away, sucker."

...Comparison and assumptions almost kept me from one of the best friendships I've ever had, because comparison and assumptions are the enemies of true friendship.

If you give in to those voices, and listen to the lies they spew, you'll be tempted to withdraw into a secluded den of isolation. But the only thing that saved me, that helped me put one foot in front of the other, was reaching out to my friends and refusing to shut up.

I would have never survived in isolation, and my faith wouldn't have either. It was out of character for me to be so chatty and open, and it might be out of character for you too, but I can tell you it makes all the difference.

God used that season of my life to teach me—an only child and introvert—what it means to live in community. I learned what it looked like to let people be part of my world, not just on a surface level, but granting them access to the most vulnerable parts of my heart.

Fortunately, I was surrounded by some seriously wonderful people who, even when I said jaw-dropping things, didn't reject me or make me feel like a lost cause. Those are the type of friends you need surrounding you. People who understand you, who know what you're saying without words, and have hope that better days are ahead for you.

When Angela found me in the pantry she didn't need an explanation. She knew exactly what was happening in my heart and mind because I didn't hide anything, including my anxiety, from her. Our friendship wasn't about perfection and polished fingernails, it was about ratty t-shirts and panic attacks. Real life. True friendship, the kind you need, is about letting someone close enough to see you in your jammies and zit cream.

Because Angela knew the real me, she knew exactly how to help me. The saddest thing about keeping people at arm's length (something I was a Jedi master at B.I.—*before India*) and not allowing them access to the messy, unpresentable parts of your life is that no one knows how to help you—or that you even need help.

However, on the flip side, the glorious part about sharing the messed-up side of ourselves, is that when you do let them in, people can help you in exactly the right ways. They can pull you out of your pit of despair and give you hope when you feel beaten so low that you can't see beyond the blades of grass on the ground where you're lying, wondering if it's worth getting up to fight again.

That's the magic of friends, no matter how dejected and hopeless you become, they still have hope for you. Good friends allow you to see yourself through their eyes for a few hours, and that's usually just long enough to get back up for another round. Be open and on the look-out. God wants to give you those types of friends.

Just to be clear, while we're on the subject of the type of friends to look for, I have a word of advice. I think we've all had friends to which we can only show the best version of ourselves. The one who turns, just as someone's about to snap a photo for Instagram, so the photographer can get their "best side." Someone we have to sanitize and edit ourselves for in order to be accepted. That is not the type of person we're looking for. Definitely not. Run screaming in the other direction from people like that, because they're not going to help you right now.

I can imagine right about now some of you might be feeling a bit jealous and wondering if you can get Angela's number because you could really use a friend like her. Some of you might even be thinking, *Well, that was nice for you. You were surrounded by supportive, loving friends and family. I'm not.*

While I can't give you Angela's number, if you're feeling lonely and isolated but ready to take a risk and find a friend, I have a few suggestions to get the ball rolling in the right direction:

Try going to a church activity. Pick someone who seems kind to sit by and strike up a casual conversation. (I know, I know, I'm killing all of you introverts right now, but this could be incredibly transformational for you. Please don't blow it off). Don't dump your story on them all at once, just see if you have a connection.

If that idea sounds too terrible, and you just groaned and made a mental list of one hundred other things you'd rather do, and one of them included cleaning the grout in your bathroom, I have another less threatening option—the internet.

An entire community of people who feel exactly the way you do could be just a click away. I've even created a safe community on Facebook where you can get started. Just search for "Faith is a Journey." We'd love to interact with you there.

One word of caution if you decide to go the virtual route. Please look for an online group of people who have hope, or are at least moving in that direction, not one that's just wallowing in feelings of self-pity and gloom. You don't need that.

There's no excuse to isolate yourself—I've debunked them all (insert maniacal laughter here). In all seriousness, if you're living in isolation there's no voice to balance out the crazy thoughts that swoop in out of the blue like a spring thunderstorm. If you hide yourself away, there's no gentle hugs or strong voices to counteract the lies that frustration and loneliness peddle. I'm telling you, you need that balance. I did. Desperately.

Our culture tells us, "You do you." With the implication that you should follow your heart. Feelings are king. But if you're honest, how often have your emotions led you astray? How often have you believed something crazy in a heightened emotional state only to discover, when you leveled out, it wasn't true at all?

The Bible warns us that our heart is deceitful above all else. Jeremiah 17:9 says,

> The human heart is the most deceitful of all things, and desperately wicked. Who really knows how bad it is? (NLT)

I don't know about you, but that doesn't sounds like something I want to trust. It sounds like following my heart and being led by my emotions will lead me towards destruction, but friends can help guide us back towards the light.

Another treasure I received from experiencing such love and acceptance from my friends and husband was how to be a friend to someone who is struggling. This season of my life softened my edges and made me more compassionate towards those who struggle, even if they struggle differently than I do. And that's something I've had to fight hard to hold on to.

As much as I wanted God to come rescue me and magically and instantly restore order to my chaos, it became increasingly clear that wasn't his plan. Instead, he offered me himself, and a pretty fantastic group of people, to walk with me through the ugly everyday when life wasn't good and I wanted to give up.

The more I study the Bible, the more clearly I see a God who chooses to come near and dwell with us in the middle of the ugly stuff. Just look at Shadrach, Meshach, and Abednego (you can find the story in Daniel 3). When they were thrown into the fiery furnace by King Nebuchadnezzar for not bowing down to worship him, God didn't choose to save them from being thrown into the fire, he joined them inside of it. The friends God placed around me were the physical representation of God's presence with me in the fiery furnace of my life.

> *The more I study the Bible, the more clearly I see a God who chooses to come near and dwell with us in the middle of the ugly stuff.*

To their credit, my friends never offered me worn-out platitudes, and they never asked me to censor my thoughts. They knew cheap words wouldn't move me. I was broken and shattered in ways no human being could mend, so Jonathan, Angela, Janna, and Jaylyn stood by and pointed to God—the only one who could fuse the broken pieces of my life back together—in their own unique ways.

It may very well be, as you move through these questions and you come out on the other side whole and healed, that you'll have the opportunity to be the friend you so desperately need right now for someone else. When that day comes, allow the wisdom that is guiding the friends who are helping you to guide you as well.

In her book Dare to Lead, Brené Brown has this advice to offer on transformative friendship: "Let go of the fear of saying the wrong thing, the need to fix it, and the desire to offer the perfect response that cures everything (that's not going to happen.)" When it comes to being a good friend she says, "You don't have to do it perfectly. Just do it."[1] We're here to help each other. Friends are what make the hard stuff just a little more bearable.

I have a recurring apocalyptic-style dream in which I'm the last remaining soul on earth. It's truly terrifying on a level that's hard to describe. Every time, I wake up in a cold sweat and I'm reminded I would rather be dead than go through life without my family and friends by my side. Don't go it alone. This isn't the apocalypse, friend, you were created to live in community.

Part 6: Does God Cause Bad Things to Happen to Us?

The way in which a man accepts his fate and all the suffering it entails, the way in which he takes up his cross, gives him ample opportunity—even under the most difficult circumstances—to add a deeper meaning to his life.

—VIKTOR FRANKL, *MAN'S SEARCH FOR MEANING*

CHAPTER FOURTEEN

Out of the Fog

Rajasthan—Fall 2009

The curves of the mossy stone structure jutting over the water arrested my attention. Its rounded turret, topped with the traditional scalloped details of Indian architecture, an abandoned artifact from a bygone Raj, was breathtaking, even in its current state of disrepair. A concrete palace, crumbling into dust, just a shadow of its former glory.

I was drawn to it in a way I couldn't explain. Snapping picture after picture, I tried to capture the feeling it evoked inside of me. It was quite literally speaking to me, but it wasn't until much later that I understood its message.

———

Our family was on a jungle safari in Ranthambore National Park, on the lookout for Bengal tigers. In no small testament to the way in which we had begun to adapt and make ourselves at home in India, it should be noted that we navigated our way to the park almost entirely by signs we read in Hindi. I hope you're sufficiently impressed. We certainly were.

Jonathan and I congratulated each other on that feat as we piled, single-file, into our small safari cart and wound our way down a well-worn jungle path. Looking back, I don't know what we were thinking, sitting in a little cart that resembled those small trains children ride in at farmer's markets, hoping to see tigers. I'm glad we didn't see any, because it would have been a terrifying encounter.

Surrounded on all sides by lush greenery, I saw a herd of deer peacefully grazing to my right and a huge tree with the most interesting branches I'd ever seen springing up from the forest floor. It reminded me of the giant tree in the center of the Animal Kingdom at Disney World. Staring agape, I wondered at the century's worth of stories hidden within its knots and twists.

For some reason, our driver decided to stop there, so we all got out. To our left, a thin concrete spillway snaked along the shore of a small lake. Jonathan and I decided to pose on the spillway for a picture. Turning to go, I froze. There, rising out of the backdrop of our picture, was the abandoned palace I described, looming in fog and drizzle. Mesmerized to the point of obsession, I found myself staring at it until it disappeared from sight.

Eventually, driving deeper into the jungle in our search for tigers, I pushed it from my mind and didn't think of it again.

Months later, I was reading Isaiah 54:11-12,14:

Afflicted city, storm-battered, unpitied:

I'm about to rebuild you with stones of turquoise,

Lay your foundations with sapphires,

construct your towers with rubies,

Your gates with jewels,

and all your walls with precious stones...

You'll be built solid, grounded in righteousness.

Immediately, the crumbling palace from our jungle safari sprung to my mind. As it did, I sensed God whisper, "It's you. That palace is a snapshot of your emotional landscape—a physical representation of how you feel inside: broken down, abandoned, and useless. But just as I promised to rebuild Israel, I want to rebuild you with beautiful, valuable stones. I know you feel like your life has crumbled to dust, but I'm remaking you into something solid, something beautiful."

> *I know you feel like your life has crumbled to dust, but I'm remaking you into something solid, something beautiful.*

Struggling to breathe, I read and reread the words of Isaiah and turned the words God had spoken to my heart over in my mind.

It seemed too good to be true that God could make something gorgeous and stunning from a pile of rubble. Those verses in Isaiah spoke of wholeness and healing, something I wanted and needed, and it called to a part of me that I thought was long dead.

As a writer, the book of Isaiah has always been one of my favorites for its vivid imagery and gorgeous use of language. Reading it this time, hope and restoration danced across the pages. Every verse breathed of it.

Even though Israel was oppressed, exiled, and seemingly abandoned, (all emotions I could identify with) God kept speaking to them about his plans for their redemption. Isaiah was saying to the Israelites, "I know it's bleak right now, but God is at work, pursuing and redeeming you in ways that aren't yet visible." It seemed he was also speaking to me, centuries later. The message? Just wait and see what I'm about to do.

CHAPTER FIFTEEN

A Wide-Angle Lens

When we were living in the Himalayan mountain village, a sweet lady named Sundri came and cooked for my helpless self four nights a week. Unfamiliar with all the fruits and vegetables piled high on the carts in the market, I needed all the help I could get.

Enter Sundri, to save us from starvation.

One afternoon, standing in the kitchen with her while she cooked, she spoke over the hiss of oil in the frying pan. "Sister, I brought this *wegetable* from the market. You'll love it." Holding out a green warty-looking zucchini in front of my eyes she said, "It's my favorite. We call it the bitter gourd." Touching her face she said, "It's so good for your skin and your blood—it makes it clean." Excited to try this super-vegetable that held such promise within such an ugly exterior, I watched her finish frying it, set it on the table, and go home for the night.

The four of us sat down to eat, and Jonathan took one look at the heaping bowl of bitter gourd that now looked like skinny, blackened octopus legs, and said, "Uh-uh. I'm not eating that."

Lifting my fork to my lips, I placed a tiny piece on my tongue. The regret was instantaneous. I looked at Jonathan, who was watching me choke it down and now had definitive evidence to support his boycott and said, "C'mon, you have to try it. I just ate it. You have to at least try it," I begged with all the logic of a demented sadist. If I was going to suffer, so was he.

Taking a giant swig of water, I tried to wash the taste out of my mouth as Jonathan continued to reject all my pleas. Apparently my words telling him it wasn't that bad weren't as convincing as my face when I ate it.

Refusing to take no for an answer, I wore him down with shameless begging until he relented. Let's just say his reaction to his first—and last—encounter with the bitter gourd was emphatic, and I was very, very sorry I made him try it.

Describing our experience with the vegetable to one of my Indian friends in Delhi, she laughed. "Ah, yes. You have to prepare the gourd," she explained. "It needs to be salted and set out in the sun to allow the bitterness to leave. You should try it again. You might like it if you prepare it correctly."

The bitter gourd turned out to be a great metaphor for our life in India. We thought it was going to be so good for us, but we didn't take the time to prepare ourselves for what we would find (at least I didn't). It wasn't until we learned how to season it, with proper perspective, that it became beneficial, even healthy.

Without the proper preparation it made me want to throw up.

A friend asked me recently if I thought God caused the circumstances that precipitated my undoing or if I thought he merely used it. It was an interesting question. One that was loaded with a kernel from every question I've addressed in this book. So the answer seemed pretty important. Monumental, even. Like the capstone of my entire Indian experience.

> *A friend asked me recently if I thought God caused the circumstances that precipitated my undoing or if I thought he merely used it.*

The more I thought about it, the more I realized I just didn't know the answer. As I wrestled and tried to discover it, I eventually came to the realization that it didn't matter. At least not to me. Because at the end of the day, whether he caused it or he used it, I was grateful. Grateful to have been utterly changed. Grateful to have a new understanding of God and my relationship with him. Grateful to finally trust his heart and intentions towards me.

If you had asked me in 2007 and 2008 if I felt grateful for all the trials and suffering I experienced I'm not sure what I would've said. Probably nothing I'd want to print here, and I'm confident "grateful" wouldn't have been the word on my lips.

But a few years later, and even now, almost a full decade removed, I can finally see the good that came from that season of my life. The struggles gave way to something beautiful, and I could see that God gave me a front row seat to watch him move in incredible ways. My wounds were healed, and I felt whole, more complete than I'd ever felt, as if pieces I never knew were missing had been restored. No more gaping holes in my heart, just scars that were gracious reminders of God's mercy and love at work in my life.

God's wide-open mercy grants us the gift of choice, to see the good or not, to choose light over dark, to move toward God or away from him, but that same freedom also allows the pain in. And even now, I still need daily reminders that beauty can come from pain.

> *God's wide-open mercy grants us the gift of choice, to see the good or not, to choose light over dark, to move toward God or away from him, but that same freedom also allows the pain in.*

For my thirtieth birthday, as a present to myself, I went to a tattoo parlor with one of my most adventurous friends and tattooed the Hindi word for love on my arm. Reminding myself, permanently, of all God has done and is still doing in my life. One of my favorite verses right now is Zechariah 2:13,

> Quiet, everyone! Silence before God. Something's afoot in his holy house. He's on the move!"

Always. You can count on it. Even when you can't see it.

When I was in the middle of it all, rats and panic attacks closing in on all sides, the only thing I could do was hang on. Just living through another day seemed like a herculean feat. I didn't have the luxury of feeling much of anything. Momentary flashes of purpose disappeared like puffs of smoke, overtaken by white-knuckle terror that if I loosened my grip for even a minute my entire life would go flying off the rails.

In a new season, where I had the benefit of time and distance to reflect on what God had done, the confluence of events and circumstances that he brought me through, the way I could see his hand at work even in my darkest moments, I could say that "grateful" summed it up perfectly.

If you're still right smack dab in the middle of the pain, unable to see anything good on your horizon and skeptical that God is at work, I understand. But as someone who's been where you are, I want to leave you with hope. I promise something good is on the way.

There's so much more happening beyond the skin of your circumstances. The trouble with, and purpose of, skin is it's designed to conceal what's beneath it. With the naked eye, we can't see what's happening beneath the surface. But just beyond our sight and our ability to comprehend, things are happening that keep us alive, healthy, and growing. It's the same with the ways in which God works in and around us. Often times his ways are concealed, just out of our sight and comprehension, but he's working nonetheless. Trust me.

There's so much more happening beyond the skin of your circumstances.

Had I written this book five years ago (and I did try), the story would have been quite different. I was still working through the process and important pieces of the puzzle were yet to come into focus. I would have written down a list of head-spinning events with no real point, because I didn't understand it all yet. Writing that book might have been helpful and cathartic for me, but I'm sure it wouldn't have been helpful for you. It would have left you scratching your head wondering why you bothered to waste your time reading it.

Maybe that's where you are right now, that painful place in your journey where nothing makes sense and meaning escapes you. Some people wander through their entire lives confused and hopeless, wrecked by their circumstances, because they never allow God to heal their wounds and shift their perspective from the pain onto himself. While I know it's incredibly tempting to camp out in that wasteland, I don't want that for you. It's not worth it. Your story, your life, is far too important to let it end that way.

Occasionally I run into a reader and they'll say something like, "Oh wow! You really went through some crazy stuff. Those rats! Ugh!" And I just nod. I don't know what to say. This story, the story God has allowed me to live, is about so much more than undesirable circumstances, anxiety, and pain. So is yours. It's about all the ways God is at work, even when it doesn't seem like it.

The most important part of this process is redemption. It's about that moment when you're whole and healed and God allows the ugliest, dirtiest, most painful parts of your story to connect with another broken, scarred soul. In a very real sense your story is your story, of course, but it may be someone else's too. Just like my story is mine, but it's not just for me. God never wastes our pain, he redeems it, often in ways that allow us to help someone else.

> *God never wastes our pain, he redeems it.*

As I write this, I have a friend who is living in India with her husband and two small children. Looking at her, I can't help but think she's living my life 8 years later. Her daughter is sick with a mysterious illness and the doctors are scratching their heads. I've watched their story unfold over Facebook from half a world away. My heart aches for her because I understand the long nights spent sitting up worrying and wondering if you'll ever get answers, or if your child will slip through your fingers while you wait.

But I know something today that I didn't know eight years ago. God is good. Full stop. Of that one thing I'm certain. In my very bones, I know that even from their dark valley, beauty will come. There will be hope, because that's the way God works.

For those of us who thrive on questions, we also like answers—and preferably ones we like. While it's frustrating to not have the answers all at once, trust the process. Trust that God is working, even when everything around you screams he's not.

I'm sure some of you might want to chalk the events that reshaped my faith up to coincidence. It was just a coincidence that Dalene shared her dream and I was there to hear it, or that Jonathan picked up a copy of *Disappointment with God* and on and on, but I believe God whispers to us in our "coincidences," giving us the opportunity to dismiss him or embrace him, to accept or reject his hand moving in our lives.

In his infinite mercy, God wrapped up one of my most nagging questions, one I've asked many times in the nine years since we returned from India. Did we miss God? Was the timing all wrong? Because I often wondered if we'd gone when the kids were older if our story would have ended differently. Would I have worried less? Would the kids have gotten so sick, since they would have been older and less likely to lick the bottom of their shoes (oh yes, you read that right)? How do you explain to a four-year-old boy that he may as well have walked into a level 4 biosafety lab and licked one of their petri dishes?

We had moved to India fully intending to spend a lifetime there, and coming home felt like failure to Jonathan and to me, each for different reasons. Him, because he'd felt called to that country since he was 17 years old, and me, because I had let him down and destroyed his dream. Those questions haunted me frequently, but I figured I'd never know the answer, until a conversation I had with a dear friend.

"You know, Erica, I have to tell you something," Jan said over the phone.

Jan was one of the youth sponsors at the church where we were youth pastors before moving to India, and she's been a close friend for a long time.

"When you and Jonathan first told us you were moving to India I was really upset," she said. "I went straight to my room and prayed that you wouldn't go. I prayed that same prayer for days until God finally rebuked me. I literally felt like he scolded me. He just said, 'No. Don't pray that anymore.'"

I could have dropped the phone for the shock that surged through my body.

It still didn't answer the "caused it or used it" question, but it definitely answered whether it was the right time and part of his plan for our family. It was part of his plan for *me*.

When we returned from India, Jonathan dove straight into college and university ministry as the state director of a ministry called Chi Alpha in Iowa. When we started in January of 2010, there were no Chi Alpha's on any campuses in Iowa, and when he resigned to become the lead pastor of Crosspoint Church in Waverly in 2014, there were nine Chi Alpha's on campuses fanned out across the state, including all the major state schools.

Jonathan and I shudder to think how we would have responded to students working through doubts and deep questions on our university campuses if we hadn't wrestled through them ourselves in India. Before India, we were woefully unprepared to address deep questions about God because we hadn't taken the time to explore them ourselves. Those three years helped us realize that questions weren't something to fear, and that embracing them could be the path to a stronger, more grounded faith.

> *Questions [aren't] something to fear, and embracing them
> could be the path to a stronger, more grounded faith.*

On a brisk fall evening in 2016, walking out of the Schindler Education Center on the University of Northern Iowa campus, where Jonathan invested four years of his life, we felt an overwhelming sense of purpose and fulfillment. It was as if we were seeing our lives from an expansive panoramic view instead of as two tiny spots through a microscope.

Each part of our journey, taken by itself, was like staring at one small section of a painting created by individual dots. When I only stared at the cluster of dots in front of my face I missed the bigger picture. Only by stepping back and looking at the entire canvas did the full masterpiece emerge. And the picture was stunning.

Thinking about the faces and stories of students impacted by Chi Alpha on campuses across Iowa, I was once again overwhelmed by the absolute goodness of God. Andy Stanley says, "Helping people view the world through the lens of Scripture is critical to providing them with the proper context from which to interpret life,"[1] and if we hadn't "failed" and returned from India, we may never have had the opportunity to do that with so many students.

The wide-angle lens, the perspective I gained as I processed the pain, a few years down the road was spectacular. Seeing the way God directed our steps was humbling, and I believe he wants to do the same for you. You might not be able to see the big picture yet, but I know it's coming. Maybe today. Maybe tomorrow.

Maybe ten years from now. I don't know when, but I know it will come.

One thing I've learned is that life is tender and fragile, and so often we think the good times will last forever. To be a real Debbie Downer, they don't. But that means the bright side of that disappointing news is that the tough times won't last forever either. It sure seems like they might sometimes, but take heart, they won't.

Too many times to count, I've wanted the road to be shorter—to skip over all the hurdles and roadblocks and be deposited straight to the finish line. Maybe that's where you are right now, but your courage is being strengthened by unimaginable degrees in the fire of pain and suffering.

> And we rejoice in the hope of the glory of God. Not only so, but we also rejoice in our sufferings, because we know that suffering produces perseverance; perseverance, character; and character, hope. And hope does not disappoint us, because God has poured out his love. (Romans 5:2-5)

It's coming my friend. Hope is coming. Hang on for one more day, one more hour, one more minute, because moment by moment, the promise of this verse is coming to life in you.

In Daniel 4, the Bible tells us about a time when King Nebuchadnezzar lost his mind. He was so deranged that he ate grass and lived outside like a wild animal for seven years. Seven. *Years.*

At the end of those seven years, God restored his sanity and his kingdom and Nebuchadnezzar praised God with this song in verse 37:

Everything he does is right, and he does it the right way. He knows how to turn a proud person into a humble man or woman.

The undoing I chronicled for you in this book was all about God getting my attention. He allowed me to experience a season of crazy, just as he did with Nebuchadnezzar, in order to wake me up. I know my heart. I know exactly where I was headed—a lifetime of religious ritual devoid of a meaningful relationship with God—and he loved me too much to let that happen.

Without the drastic measures and extremes of India I may have "served God" my whole life, but never truly experienced him. I could have worked for my salvation for an entire lifetime and never understood the extravagance of God's free gift of grace and love. It took India, in all of her brutal glory, for God to show me who I really was and what I truly believed about him.

Is it possible that God is trying to get your attention? Could the circumstances or "coincidences" of your life be God reaching out to you, offering a greater understanding of himself and his love for you? Could the pain you're experiencing be an invitation to depths you've never plumbed before?

> *Is it possible that God is trying to get your attention? Could the circumstances or "coincidences" of your life be God reaching out to you?*

I believe it is.

What are the "coincidences" in your life that are whispering of God? Will you accept them and allow God to use your story and your experiences to answer your questions?

God is writing a beautiful story with your life. He uses the bitter with the sweet, the light with the dark, the joy alongside the pain to create meaning that's often beyond our ability to comprehend or even appreciate. He is writing *his* story with your life, and he is a master at taking the most devastating plot twists and forming beauty from the ashes.

It's been almost a decade since my story began, and it's taken nearly that long to sort through it all. To finally reach a place where I can see goodness in the pain, joy in the sorrow, and blessings amidst the broken bits. Welcome to the journey, friend. I'm here, and so is God. Waiting. Will you ask the honest questions and listen for the small voice that answers back? If so, you're on your way to *holy* doubt.

Part 7: Beyond Holy Doubt

God is best known in not knowing him.

—SAINT AUGUSTINE

CHAPTER SIXTEEN

Reclaiming the Wonder

If you've made it this far there's one more thing we need to talk about. Mystery. Because that little word has the power to throw us for a huge loop if we stumble upon it unprepared.

Doubt and mystery are two sides of a similar coin. If we wrestle well with our doubts, it stands to reason we might also do well with mystery. But the opposite can be true. Like doubt, mystery has the potential to destroy us, but handled properly it can give us an even richer experience with, and deeper understanding, of God.

It's all in how you process it.

The church I grew up in had a magnificent closet in the basement Fellowship Hall. As you descended the stairs from the main level the wood slatted door to your left led you into a giant tunnel crammed full of extra tables and chairs. If you entered through that magical portal, you were transported via secret passageway to the Fellowship Hall. With doors on both ends, that storage area was glorious beyond description (unless you happened to be "it" during our games of tag, because those two exits made it nearly impossible to catch anyone!) It was the best hiding place for hide and seek, and the stuff of squirrelly children's dreams. I spent many joyful hours of my life running through that closet.

But there was another closet, tucked deep behind the stage, that I tried to avoid. It was stuffed to overflowing with cast-off props from Easter and Christmas productions gone by, and dusty old decorations that had probably been around since the days of Methuselah. It honestly creeped me out. It was a mess; full of forgotten relics no one wanted to talk about or use anymore.

I think doubt and mystery can be a lot like that second closet. We'd like to leave them in the dark recesses, unexplored and forgotten, but in doing so, we have the potential to miss so much.

More and more conversations about doubt are being started across so many different mediums, and I'm so excited to see it happening. If ever there was a time to wrestle well with our doubts and questions, it's now. We're just beginning to bring doubt out into the open and talk about it in a healthy way. I've heard more and more people willing to speak out about their own dark night of the soul, and a number of books have come out exploring doubt and faith questions.

> *If ever there was a time to wrestle well with our doubts and questions, it's now.*

Mystery too has been addressed for centuries by everyone from Biblical authors to Augustine and

Aquinas. But there's one part of mystery that's still lurking in the dark corners of that second closet, the one nobody wants to get into, and not many people want to bring it out of the shadows.

We all want to talk about the wonder-filled side of mystery, but no one wants to talk about the shadowy underbelly. When God's mysterious nature isn't just puzzling, it's painful.

Right now I'd like to state the obvious. God is a mystery. And that one statement makes all of us uncomfortable to one degree or another. Some of us more. Some of us less. But I'd venture to say it makes every last one of us feel just a bit anxious deep in our core.

If he's a mystery, it means he doesn't always move the way we want, or in ways we can predict. And he's not bound by the same rules. That can be scary. So we'd like to strip him of his mysterious nature, thank you very much. Especially if you're a control freak like me. Just go back over some of the previous chapters if you want evidence of said need to control.

Humans don't like mystery. We don't like things we can't explain. We've been trying to unravel the mysteries of the universe ever since we drew our very first collective breath.

Whenever something goes wrong, someone gets sick, or a business fails, we want to know why. We launch an inquisition, an exploratory committee, or a medical trial, to discover the source of the error or the unknown virus or bacteria that caused the disease. Don't get me wrong. This thirst for knowledge has served us quite well on various fronts. Science, medicine, you get the idea. While many of the results of these attempts to explore

144 | ERICA BARTHALOW

the mysterious corners of life have been wildly beneficial, I think it's robbed us of something essential where
it relates to God.

If we're honest, I think way down deep in our souls
we feel if we study hard enough, we'll finally figure God
out. That there's a secret code to crack, and suddenly he
will just make sense.

> *Way down deep in our souls we feel if we study hard enough,*
> *we'll finally figure God out.*

And we're disappointed when that doesn't happen.

We're crushed when his character and his plans defy
our explanations and our ability to comprehend. So we
think there must be something wrong with God, or at
least our relationship with him.

There is.

We're uncomfortable with an essential part of the
very nature of God.

Our mistake is assuming that God is like us. And we
consciously or unconsciously do this because that's all
our brains can really understand. It's the only thing we
have a category for. But God exists outside of our understanding and our categories. We don't even possess the
ability to fully understand him. There is no frame of ref-
erence for him.

In the early 2000's the phrase "Jesus is my homeboy"
started popping up everywhere, and was embraced coast
to coast by all kinds of people. You could even find

celebrities wearing t-shirts with the slogan splashed across their chests.

Towards the beginning of the book, I mentioned I grew up in the 80's and 90's with a Jonathan Edwards "Sinners in the hands of an angry God" theology. There wasn't much talk of God's grace and mercy, it was mainly all judgment, all the time. At least that's the way I remember it.

But somewhere in the late 90's and early 2000's I think we rode the pendulum to the other extreme. Now we hear an awful lot about God's love and mercy, but very little about his judgment and righteousness. We started calling Jesus our "homeboy," making him familiar and accessible, but nearly abandoning his just and righteous nature.

That's where we're missing it. It's not an either/or, it's a both/and situation. And when we lose any part of God's true nature, we don't treat him with the wonder and reverence he deserves. And we get uncomfortable with the mystery.

> *When we lose any part of God's true nature, we don't treat him with the wonder and reverence he deserves.*

Pastor Tom Clegg from The Gateway Church in Des Moines says a paradox "affirms the truth of two opposing ideas that cannot be logically reconciled. Such truth [of the two opposing ideas together] is greater than either of the two sides of the paradox."[1]

I don't know that many of us are content to dwell in the mystery of God—within his paradoxical nature. The God who is near and yet far, unknowable and yet familiar? I defies our ability to comprehend and it makes us squirm.

Often we grant more freedom to our friends and spouse to maintain an aura of mystique and mystery than we allow God. We find it intriguing, or even alluring, with others but offensive with God.

> *Often we grant more freedom to our friends and spouse to maintain an aura of mystique and mystery than we allow God.*

In his devotional *Every Step an Arrival*, Eugene Peterson writes, "We are constantly reminded and inevitably impressed with our power. We can do nearly anything we want. No longer bound to the cycles of the seasons, we create our own heat in winter and cold in summer. No longer restricted by the natural rhythms of night and day, we produce our own light and work where we will."[2]

It's as if we're saying to God, "We've got this. We don't need your plans anymore. Our ways are better. We've got it all figured out."

I think we've come to believe that the mysteries of the universe are owed to us. We feel entitled to knowledge, and we're upset if it's withheld from us. And that attitude has bled into our relationship with God. The Creator of the universe. Putting it down in black and white, it's almost laughable.

And yet...

We live in a culture that demands transparency, and if a company or person is unwilling to give it, we are immediately suspicious. We wonder, *what are they hiding?* We don't generally ascribe good motives to such behavior. Usually for good reason. More often than not, a lack of transparency in government or the corporate world is covering something up, some wrongdoing, because we're dealing with flawed, imperfect people.

To harbor the same suspicious attitude towards God and the mystery that surrounds him would be a mistake, though. Because he's not part of a massive cover-up, or trying to keep us from discovering his true nature. On the contrary, he's revealed his nature to us already.

The ancients seemed to be far more comfortable with mystery. They lived hand-in-hand with it, even found comfort in it. Some would probably say that's because they had to.

We, on the other hand, have unlocked the secrets buried within our genetic code; even predicting if someone is likely to get cancer or carries a certain hereditary disease. Discoveries made from hours spent crouched in a lab, hunched over a microscope discovering things previously unknown to the minds of human beings, has hatched an insatiable desire to know more, to wrap our minds around the biggest mysteries of our time. But generations past didn't have the knowledge and access that modern science and technology have given to us. Our ancestors lived with a much greater deficit of knowledge. There was no Google, MIT, or anything of the sort.

And yet, with all of the advancements we've made and all the things we've demystified, do we have a greater appreciation for mystery, or less?

I think we believe if we just study a bit harder, investigate a little further, we'll somehow reveal everything there is to know about everything—including God. As preposterous as it sounds, I think subconsciously we truly believe that. It was the root of Adam and Eve's sin; they wanted to become like God and possess his knowledge. So many, many years later nothing has changed.

The trouble is, what if we were never meant to know everything? What if mystery is the very thing that draws us towards God and makes us dependent on him? And if that's true, and God longs to draw us to him, then the most loving thing he's done is conceal and keep some things hidden from us.

> *What if mystery is the very thing that draws us towards God and makes us dependent on him?*

As a kid I always hated being left out of the loop. When somebody had vital information and purposely excluded me, it hurt. I especially hate it as an adult. And I really don't like it when it seems like God is withholding information from me.

I'm sure we've all found ourselves left in the dark "for our own good" at one point or another. It reminds me of the time I was in labor with my son, completely out of it on Fentanyl, and my mom, thinking I was asleep, whispered to my husband, "Don't tell Erica, but her grandma isn't doing well."

I wanted to know that information. I didn't need to be shielded from it. But there are other times when I've been protected from something and I appreciated it.

Proverbs 25:2 says,

> It is God's privilege to conceal things
>
> and the king's privilege to discover them.

My two kids, now teenagers, are always asking me why. Considering what I shared earlier in the book, that seems fair and probably inevitable, right? Touché! I guess I'm getting a taste of my own medicine. But sometimes the why my kids are seeking isn't helpful to them. Sometimes it doesn't matter why.

It's God's prerogative to reveal or conceal. What if the information and answers being kept from you really are for your own good? I think the biblical character Job can offer us some insight here. The book of Job both comforts and disturbs me.

We'll get to the comforting part in a minute, but let's just dive in to the disturbing part. That part of the mystery of God that can feel painful to us.

I find Job disturbing because it so clearly breaks down the dichotomy between what I feel I have the right to know and what I'm allowed to know. And if I'm honest, the few answers that God gives Job isn't enough for me. It leaves me with even more questions than it answers.

As hard as I try, I can't get over the fact that God allowed all of Job's children to be wiped away. And even though he eventually gave him more children, as a parent, there's no explanation for the loss of his other children that makes sense. The pain would be too raw, too real. It's something I would never get over. And God doesn't really give us a reason, other than Job's testing. Which to my limited understanding, hardly seems worth it.

There are so many things in this life that defy any reasonable explanation. The tragic and unexpected death of a young parent. A devastating diagnosis. God could give us a reason, yes, but it wouldn't make it any easier to swallow. It would still hurt just as much. It wouldn't change the lonely ache the young widow feels when she looks at her fatherless children, or the uncertainty and fear in the one with an incurable cancer diagnosis.

Mystery is the thing that causes us to ask the difficult questions that may not have an answer, or at least one we can accept. And that makes many in the church uncomfortable. Hence, the reason why we don't like to talk about it. We don't like to admit we don't have all the answers.

In 1991, Garth Brooks' song, "Unanswered Prayers" was at the top of the Billboard charts. I was 10. A few years later, as a teenager, I remember joking around and singing the chorus of the song at church with some friends and being scolded, "God always answers. Sometimes his answer is just no, or wait." Alrighty then. I think we were just messing around. But I remember taking those words as gospel.

However, the more I've experienced and the more I think about it, I'm convinced life just isn't that black and white. Sometimes, there are no answers.

At the end of the book of Job, God doesn't really give Job any solid answers. Instead, he kind of puts him in his place. His response to Job reminds me of some conversations I've had with my teenagers. He says, "Were you there when I created the world? No? Okay then. Maybe you don't understand what's really going on here" (my paraphrase). And since he doesn't give any answers, perhaps the point of the book isn't answers at all, but something else. To prove that God is beyond our understanding? That he doesn't owe us an explanation? To start a conversation with us? To inspire awe and reverence?

But even if we can acknowledge that God is beyond our understanding, we do still long for the mysteries of God to be unveiled.

Matthew 27:51 says,

> At that moment [when Jesus died on the cross] the curtain in the sanctuary of the Temple was torn in two, from top to bottom." (NLT)

For a long time the significance of that sentence eluded me. We have to travel back to the Old Testament to truly understand the wonder that one sentence contains.

Before Jesus' sacrifice for us, humans were unable to enter the presence of God. They were separated from him and his presence by the veil leading to the Holy of Holies, and only the high priest was able to enter once a year. But at the very moment Jesus died, the veil separating us from his presence was ripped in half. Granting us access to the presence of God that no human being had ever experienced before in history.

But we still want more.

Even that term "unveiling" seeks to remove a bit of the mystery. In an effort to draw near to us, God tore the veil separating us from his holy presence. However, that act didn't change the essence of who he is. He is still the same holy, separate, mysterious being he was before. He's just allowed us to draw near.

So, how do we learn to live within the tension of the revealed and the mystery, the known and the unknowable? And why does it even matter? I'm glad you asked.

Being comfortable with the mystery of God is important because if we don't get comfortable with it, it will robs us of joy and peace and breeds distrust. And distrust often leads to misunderstandings.

When we're uncomfortable with mystery we start telling ourselves stories that may or may not be true. The root behind all of our attempts to explain away the mystery, to uncover the hidden things of God, is fear. Fear of the unpredictable. Fear of the unknown. Fear of not knowing what we should be afraid of.

> *The root behind all of our attempts to explain away the mystery, to uncover the hidden things of God, is fear.*

It's in the process of confronting that fear, and naming it, that we can start moving towards the wonder of mystery. We can choose to recapture the wonder of God's mystery, rather than fearing it.

I'm going to circle back to a statement I made earlier. What if the mystery of God is really the very thing that draws you towards him? If that's true, it would be the most loving thing for him to maintain it.

I know you're going to be surprised that I've got a few questions for you to think on. These are things I've been wrestling with myself. So, let's get really personal for a minute.

- How do you respond to things unknown?
- Are you comfortable sitting with it? Really?
- Do you immediately search for answers? Start asking questions?
- Do you have to know everything?
- Does knowing everything from start to finish change the outcome?
- What if not knowing, instead of being a point of shame or frustration, was instead a point of comfort?
- If you could understand everything about God, would you still want to follow him?
- Would you trust him with your life?
- Does it make you feel less secure, or more secure, to know that scientists don't know what the farthest reaches of the galaxies contain, but God does?
- Are you going to feel comfortable trusting your life to someone who doesn't know any more about the future than you do?

Imagine with me that you know everything. No thing is outside of your deep well of knowledge. Would you feel complete? Satisfied? Or would you feel let down?

Disappointed, even? That the universe was small enough for you to comprehend.

I don't know about you, but the conclusions I've reached about those questions give me a sense of comfort as I settle into the mystery of God. A sense of peace and trust in the future and the One who holds it.

I've tried very hard not to offer "churchy" answers or tidy advice to such a complex and difficult subject. But the hard truth is, as much as we often don't like it, and we can't understand it, God just doesn't work the way we do. And much of what he does, and allows, we will never have explained in this life.

Which leads us to our response.

How do we move past the fear? How do we find a way to live well within the mysterious tension of a God beyond our comprehension?

CHAPTER SEVENTEEN

Sinking into the Mystery

Have you ever watched someone struggle against quicksand? It was a popular plot tool in old Western movies. The music would turn dark and dramatic as our hero, no doubt wearing a cowboy hat and boots, unwittingly walked or fell into a well-camouflaged vat of soupy soil.

Then the struggle began.

Sometimes the cowboy made it out and sometimes he didn't. The phrase from Star Trek, spoken in a robotic accent, "Resistance is futile," comes to mind. Generally, the harder the character fought, the more likely they were to get sucked under.

The same can be true as we wrestle with doubt and mystery. The more we struggle against it, the more likely it is to destroy us. And we can easily drag others down with us.

It's the struggle that sucks you under.

So how do you sink into the mystery of God like a comfy feather bed, rather than fighting it like quicksand? In a word: trust. The other five letter word (because doubt has five letters too—in case you were confused).

Author and pastor Francis Chan, in his Bible study of the book of James,[1] said he prays for God to refine him through trials and suffering so that he can more clearly reflect Christ. Say what now?

When I heard him say that I cringed.

My knee-jerk response to pain, hurt, and suffering, even after everything I've experienced, is still "No way! No thank you!" I think that makes me a normal human being. But I've also learned those very things are often what bring growth and a deeper relationship with God.

So if I drill down and really examine my response it comes down to my level of trust. Do I trust that any pain, heartache, or suffering that God allows to come my way will ultimately be for my good? Do I trust that he truly has my good in mind?

When the hard times (or even the potential for hard times) come, my true feelings about God come bubbling to the surface. I can't hide them. Either I believe God is good and trustworthy, or I don't. All is revealed in my response.

When I pause long enough to really think it through, I know God is more than worthy of my trust, but I still find it hard to pray like Francis Chan did. Because there's still that element of the unknown, of what it will cost. And I'm usually wondering if it will be more than I'm willing to pay.

As I watched Francis Chan talk about his desire to more clearly and accurately reflect Jesus no matter the cost, I again recognized how far I still have to go and that on some level I still distrust God and the goodness of his plans for me. What joy and richness have I forfeited in order to be safe and secure and continue down my comfortable path of routine? How many times have I missed an opportunity to reflect Jesus to those around me?

Ultimately, it all comes back to trust. Sigh. Wouldn't it be nice if learning to trust was a one-time-fixes-all experience (while we're wishing for things, I also wish paying taxes was a one-time-covers-all deal too). Instead, it seems to be a daily choice. But if I trust God, I can pray that scary prayer that Francis Chan prayed and know that whatever he gives me is for my good and his glory.

Since this is a revised version of the book, I've had the opportunity to hear from quite a few readers. People who are hurting deeply, wondering where in the world God is in the midst of their pain. They want answers. I wanted answers too. They don't want to live within the tension of mystery and yet unanswered questions. They want resolution to their difficult circumstances. I get it. I really do.

Our society is uncomfortable with pain. We try to avoid it all costs. The opioid epidemic is all the evidence we need to confirm that this is true. Millions have gone to desperate lengths, even spiraling into addiction, to numb the pain and dull their feelings.

We have a hard time understanding how painful events can work for our good. It is definitely one of the most confounding paradoxes in Scripture. We get upset with God and lose faith in him because we have different views on pain and suffering. Perhaps the fault isn't with God though. Can I open your heart to the idea that maybe we've just misunderstood God's purpose?

What if the point of pain is to get your attention? What if the intersection of your pain and desperation is the spot where God is longing to speak to you? Where he's longing to reveal himself through you?

> *What if the point of pain is to get your attention?*

Life can seem unfair in the middle of intense trials and suffering, but God isn't always concerned about the same things we are. If that statement upset you, hang with me for just a minute while I explain.

Haggai 2:17 says,

> I [the Lord] sent blight and mildew and hail to destroy everything you worked so hard to produce. Even so, you refused to return to me, says the Lord. (NLT)

To us, or at least to me (I won't speak for you), that seems terrible. The idea that God would destroy the work of our hands is offensive. But what if he's willing to go scorched earth because he's after something much greater than our prosperity? What if he's after our hearts? And revealing his glory to those far from him?

John 11 tells an interesting story about a man named Lazarus. Jesus receives word that his good friend Lazarus is near death. And even though Jesus could have traveled immediately to Lazarus' bedside and halted his death, he waited. He did this so that God's glory could be displayed in an incredible way. But you can hear the pain and echo of disappointment in Martha's words in verse 21, "'Lord, if only you had been here, my brother would not have died." She, like us, knew he had the power to prevent her pain, but chose not to.

Even when he can spare us pain, there are times when he doesn't, and that can be really hard to stomach. But it's always because there is a greater purpose afoot just beyond our sight or understanding.

Psalm 100:3 says,

> Know this: God is God, and God,
>
> God.
>
> He made us; we didn't make him.
>
> We're his people, his well-tended
>
> sheep.

This verse reminds me who God is, and that I'm not him. He is the creator. I am not. He alone is sovereign. That's a fancy word we like to toss around to make it easier to shut down hard questions. We can just say with a little shrug, "Well, God is sovereign." Meaning he can do what he likes, when he likes, how he likes, and don't bother trying to explain it.

But I think we have a hard time swallowing this idea about God's sovereignty because we forget that the earth and everything in it belongs to him.

Psalm 24:1 tells us,

> The earth is the Lord's, and everything in it.
>
> The world and all its people belong to him.

We feel like our families and our bank accounts and our careers all belong to us. When our lives are clicking along predictably, we're tricked into believing we have a modicum of control. And this idea of God's sovereignty disturbs our illusion of control. But the earth and everything, and everyone, in it belongs to him.

He was, and is, the originator of it all.

That doesn't mean we're not allowed to have feelings about what he does. But we aren't given a vote.

Imagine with me for a moment that Shakespeare is still alive and well, still cranking out some of the greatest literary works known to man. But let's say in an artistic fit he decided to destroy all of his work—every last word. Robbing us, and generations to come, of his creative genius. Most of us would feel sadness at such a great loss, and many of us would have questions. But the work belongs to him. He created it, and he has the right to do with it whatever he chooses.

So it is with God, to a much greater degree.

We are certainly allowed our emotions. We can feel anger, sadness, loss, and sorrow at his actions, but his work (i.e. us, the world) belongs to him and he is free to do what he deems best.

It's so easy to forget that the people and things we love don't really belong to us. Again, I have to remind myself: The earth is the Lord's, and everything in it. My family belongs to God, and the ways in which he works with and through them is ultimately designed to bring about their ultimate good and give him glory.

In *It's Not Supposed to be This Way*, Lysa TerKeurst writes, "To fix our thoughts on Jesus is to close our eyes. To mark this moment by declaring our trust in God...to stop fixating on the circumstances raging around us. To stop trying to make sense of things that make no sense in the middle of the journey. And to stop asking for the knowledge that's too heavy for us to carry."

Going on she says, "We are so quick to judge the quality of our lives and the reliability of God based on individual events rather than the eventual good God is working on putting together."[2]

What if the ugliest circumstance in your life right now is exactly the spot where God is going to reveal his glory? What if God is better than we ever dreamed or thought possible? What if his plans are better than ours? Seriously, take a minute to contemplate those questions. The answers just might rock your world.

> *What if God is better than we ever dreamed or thought possible?*

Do you like surprises? As far as I'm concerned, there are two types of people in the world: those who like surprises and those who don't. The latter are bent on ruining every Christmas and birthday surprise—you know who you are (and you should be ashamed of yourselves, just kidding—sort of). My husband is one of these people. He goes to great lengths to spoil any and all of my surprises, and it drives me crazy. On the other hand, he could wrap a present for me in the same room and I wouldn't peek because I love surprises! I think God laughs when two people who share these opposite traits get together. So what do your opinions about surprises have to do with doubt and mystery? Good question.

In some small way, your feelings about surprises can predict how you'll interact with God and respond to the mystery that surrounds him. Because our feelings about surprises can be directly linked to the level of trust we feel towards the giver of the surprise.

Can we flip the mystery of God from a thing of discomfort and fear, to a state of excitement and anticipation? John and Lisa Bevere have said that wilderness seasons (times of pain and suffering) are the preparation ground for a promise on the horizon.[3] Can we learn to look beyond the surface of events and circumstances that seem difficult and devastating, and see the coming victory? Can we reframe our pain and suffering as a stop along our journey, not our final destination?

If we can learn to look at mystery through that lens, we can be content knowing that while God may be concealing details from us now, we can trust that he is up to something good.

Recently, I joined a CrossFit gym. I'm still dumbfounded that I can even write that sentence. When a friend first asked if I'd like to join, I laughed in her face. I don't lift weights. I like exercises like pilates and yoga where I don't break a sweat. But in a moment of pure insanity I decided to check it out. And to my deep surprise, I loved it.

It just so happens that CrossFit is a great metaphor for trust. Just like I'm building muscle in the gym day by day, and one day I'll be lifting and doing things I never dreamed possible, my faith builds up a little day by day too. Each time I experience God's faithfulness, trusting him becomes easier and easier. But also like weight training, as we get comfortable and complacent where we are, we have to keep pushing past our comfort level to see improvement and changes. It's been hard, but so good—in the gym, and in learning to trust.

I asked the question earlier: how do we live in the tension of what we see and what we'll never see this side of eternity? In the now and not yet? In our reality and the mystery?

Simply put, trust.

In *Hope in the Dark*, Craig Groeschel writes, "If you had everything figured out, you wouldn't need faith. You could live simply by your understanding. By your logic, but not by faith. But when you don't understand something, that gives you the unique opportunity to deepen your faith. Oswald Chambers said, 'Faith is deliberate confidence in the character of God whose ways you may not understand at the time.'"[4]

I said earlier in the book that one of the platitudes I embraced before India opened my eyes was, "God will never give you more than you can handle." I think it came from a misinterpretation of 1 Corinthians 10:13 where it says, "...God is faithful. He will not allow the temptation to be more than you can stand. When you are tempted, he will show you a way out so that you can endure."

There's a subtle word choice there that caused me to believe something that wasn't there. God promises we will never be tempted beyond what we can bear. But that verse never promised I wouldn't find myself in overwhelming circumstances, experiencing more than I could mentally or emotionally handle. In fact, I've come to learn that God frequently gives me more than I can handle, because he doesn't expect me to "handle" it at all. He wants me to come to him, rest in him, and trust him to handle it.

That's the big secret about the way God works. And it's not even a well-kept one. It's splashed all over the pages of the Bible. For years and years I was just too dense to see it. Every line of every story, in the Bible and the stories he's writing with our individual lives, has been about our hearts. It's always been about our hearts. From the very beginning. Even when he seems cruel and inscrutable—God is pursuing our hearts. Through any means that will get our attention.

> *Every line of every story, in the Bible and the stories he's writing with our individual lives, has been about our hearts.*

Can you trust, even when God is wrapped up tight in mystery and life hurts, that a God who would go through such lengths, throughout all of human history, to get to you is trustworthy? Will you be able to say it is good? That *he* is good? Even when your circumstances don't seem good or feel good?

1 Peter 4:12-13 says,

> Dear friends, don't be surprised at the fiery trials you are going through, as if something strange were happening to you. Instead, be very glad—for these trials make you partners with Christ in his suffering, so that you will have the wonderful joy of seeing his glory when it is revealed to all the world.

Did you catch that? He's making us partners with Christ in the hard times, when it's confusing and sometimes hard to trust. We are partners with Christ. I don't know about you, but that blows my mind.

And it definitely gives me hope when things seem bleak and uncertain.

In *God Where Are You?* John Bevere writes, "Praise will cause your focus to turn from you to the Lord. In the midst of trials, it is easy to lose sight of the ability of God because of the intense pressure we face. David wrote the majority of his Psalms in the middle of trials. By praising God, he was able to stay strong in really adverse circumstances."[5]

The same thing that carried David through is what will carry you and me through too. Turning our attention away from what's before our eyes and onto the mesmerizing wonder that is the mystery of God.

Walking the path of doubt and mystery can sometimes make us skeptical about every part of a relationship with Jesus—including talking to him. We can find ourselves not only skeptical about the character of God, but also whether he really hears us or will answer us. So we don't pray. Or when we do pray, we're surprised when he answers.

I want to throw down a challenge right here, right now. Pray. Ask God to give you the ability to trust him in the middle of whatever has turned your world upside down and caused you to doubt his character, the very fabric of His goodness. You might not feel like it, and you might even wonder if it will make a difference. I'm not going to lie, it may not make any discernible difference at all to your circumstances, but it will change you. If even just for a few moments, it will lift your eyes off of what's immediately before you and comfort you with God's eternal perspective.

Here's something to cling to as you trust that God has you right where he wants you in order to do something in and through you that you never would have believed possible. It brought me to tears. In his book *Didn't See it Coming,* Carey Nieuwhof writes, "If God wants to go deep, it's because he wants to take you far."[6]

If you're wrestling with doubt and mystery, my friend, it is deep work. But have hope! God wants to grow you, develop you, and increase your capacity, because he wants to take you far. He has greater things in store. Good things. Things that will blow your mind.

Get ready.

Epilogue

I hope this book began a journey for you—a process. That's the word that God is speaking to me, even now. Process. And two others—passionate patience. I've never been a patient person, and I've definitely never been passionate about waiting. But some things are worth the wait. Seeing this process through, along with the profound changes it brings, is well worth the wait. I would love to hear how God is working in your life. Drop me a note and tell me what God is up to. I'd love to hear your story. You can email me at: erica@droppingtheact.com.

Recommended Reading

1. *Disappointment with God.* Philip Yancey

2. *Crazy Love.* Francis Chan

3. *The Ragamuffin Gospel* (visual edition). Brennan Manning

4. *Where is God When It Hurts?* Philip Yancey

5. *Bittersweet.* Shauna Niequist

6. *The Shack.* William Paul Young

7. *Hope in the Dark.* Craig Groeschel

8. *It's Not Supposed to be This Way.* Lysa TerKeurst

9. *Where are you God?* John Bevere

10. *Job* and *Isaiah.* The Bible

Acknowledgments

We all carry pieces of a beautiful story inside of us. The act of writing is an effort to share those stories with the world. My unending thanks to these beautiful souls who allowed me to share a piece of their stories within these pages, and/or walked with me through mine: Dalene, Angela and Chad, Jeannie, Paul, Jaylyn and Brice, Rachel and Hannah, Janna, Monique, Charlotte, Jan, Vanessa, Paul and Shelley, Brian and Leslie, Tim and Liz, Joey and Carla, Caroline, Jerad, Dilip, Nick and Marcae, Barbra and Jerry, Cheryl, Rebecca and all of our precious Indian brothers and sisters (who I won't mention by name, as not to cause unnecessary trouble, but you know who you are).

To my dad, who was the first to show me that the path toward a fuller relationship with God can lead through doubt. Thanks for always being ready with some interesting questions. Love you!

For my mom, who thinks everything I do is amazing and single-handedly told all of North America about this book. You are wonderful. Love you!

For Jonathan, words fail. I'm the luckiest woman on the face of the planet to get to call you mine. You were, and are, my safe spot, my center. Outside of Jesus, no other love has changed me so completely. Life with you is the sweetest adventure. ILUM.

To Jacob and Juliana, I count being your mom as one of the greatest privileges of my life. I love each of you completely and uniquely, and having a front row seat to watch you grow has been a gift beyond description. My prayer is that someday, if you find yourselves on the stormy seas of doubt, you'll find comfort in these words and a light for your path.

India, you're an indelible part of my story, and you've rewritten my life and faith with a richness I never could have anticipated. I'll be forever grateful.

For Tom and Lori and Heath and Ali, thank you for providing a safe place for us to land when we came home from India broken and hurting. You played a pivotal role in allowing us space to heal. For that, we count you as dear friends.

To Mike and Paul and our Chi Alpha friends, you were exactly the community we needed to be part of when we came back from India. Thanks for being so unspeakably wonderful to us!

A special shout out to Kendall Davis and Jan Soults Walker for their amazing editing skills and countless hours spent helping me craft a story that makes sense. I appreciate it more than you know.

Thank you Angela, Jaylyn, Leslie, Shelley, and Janna for living the "ugly everyday" with me. I couldn't have asked for better friends. You were the very picture of love when I needed it most.

And to the many friends who supported me on the long journey of writing this story down, who prayed for me when my brain hurt and was overwhelmed with thoughts of: "I can't do this": Jenn, Jennie, Carolyn, Anna, Jan, Vanessa. You guys are rockstars. And for the incredible book launch team that signed on to help spread this message: Julie, Jennie, Sonia, Amy, Sarah, Jenny, Sam, Sara, Marissa, Angela, Jan, Lori, Hannah, Carolyn, Danica, Vanessa, Christi, Kerri, Kimberly, Elizabeth, Jonathan, Janet, Heather, Dianna, Jenn, Anna, Susan, Lisa, Alyssa, Cherise, Erin, Nichole, Brenda, Heidi, Lori, Cindi, Ronda, Mallory, Heather, Angie, Diane, Hannah, Dee, Danielle, Renee, Kristy, and Elisia. You're the absolute best! Thanks for all the love and support.

And finally, in the tradition of Bach, Soli Deo Gloria—To the Glory of God Alone. I only want to live a story that brings you glory, always.

Questions for Reflection and/or Discussion

CHAPTER 1

1. Have you ever found yourself questioning God's goodness?
2. If so, what life circumstances brought about those questions?
3. Have you ever felt abandoned by God? What happened to make you feel that way?
4. Hopelessness and despair can cause us to do things we many not otherwise ever consider. Have you ever felt so hopeless that you couldn't see an end to your suffering?

*A note from Erica:
At the beginning of "Abandoned" I was contemplating suicide because I felt God had left me and I didn't think there would ever be an end to the unbearable hopelessness I felt. If that's you today, if that describes how you feel, please know that even though it feels like your life will never change, like you're stuck in a horrible version

of *Groundhog's Day*, it won't last forever. Things will change. As someone who has been there and felt those same feelings, I want you to know there's hope and life won't always be like this. Hang on and *tell someone how you're feeling today!*

CHAPTER 2

1. Have you ever had an unwelcome clash between your expectations and reality?
2. How did you cope with that experience?
3. Do you notice a connection between your anxiety and stress levels and your sense of purpose? How do those two elements interact with one another in your life?
4. Have you ever struggled through a season where it seemed God was silent? How did you respond?
5. What did you think about the "once saved, never saved" theology that Erica grew up with? What do you think that means?
6. Did you grow up with a similar background and view of God?
7. Have you ever believed that you needed to behave a certain way in order to make God happy with you? Why or why not?

CHAPTER 3

1. Have you ever found yourself so knotted up with pain and disappointment that you didn't recognize the person you'd become?
2. Did feeling that way motivate you to change or cause you to sink deeper into despair? Why?

3. How did you feel when you read the story of Dalene's dream about the shale wall and the strawberry patch?

4. What are your strawberry patches? Are there things in your life, like Dalene's strawberry patch, that God is reminding you about? Things he has placed in your life to display his desire to delight you, not frustrate and hurt you?

5. Erica realized in this chapter that she assumed she was alone in feeling frustrated and angry with God. What important truths about being honest about our relationship with God can we draw from this chapter?

6. Erica asked several questions at the end of this chapter that are worth contemplating and discussing. They are:
   - Did she and God have different definitions of the word "good"?
   - What does it mean that joy and delight can be found in the midst of intense suffering?

CHAPTER 4

1. Erica "coincidentally" found herself at a church where the pastor had copies of *Disappointment with God* to give away. Are there "coincidences" in your life that are pointing towards God's love and pursuit of you?

2. What images are brought to your mind when you hear God described as the "Hound of Heaven"? What do you think the poet meant by describing God this way?

CHAPTER 5

1. Erica asks the question, "Could there be more behind my experiences?" If you're currently going through a difficult experience, could there be more (more to learn about yourself, about God, about your story) underneath the skin of your experiences that you haven't discovered yet?
2. What role do physical things (like getting enough rest) play in helping us process our experiences in a healthy way?
3. Are you ever tempted to withhold your true thoughts and feelings from God? Why or why not?
4. Share your thoughts about this statement: "Any answer to the question "Why?" will never be enough to fill up our empty spaces and erase the scars of pain and suffering?" Do you think that's true or not?
5. Learning to ask a new questions: "To what end?" became a catalyst in Erica's faith journey. How might that question help you in yours?

CHAPTER 6

1. Have you ever prayed a "dangerous prayer"? What was the result?
2. Have you ever felt dissatisfied with your relationship with God and wondered if there was more? What did you do?

CHAPTER 7

1. Sometimes there is a stigma attached to counseling. What are your feelings about it?

2. If you have prayed a dangerous prayer, would you have still prayed it if you had known what the answer would be?

3. What did you think when Jeanne told Erica she had been given a gift—she just need to figure out how to unwrap it?

4. How is your interpretation of the events and experiences you've gone through influencing your thoughts about God? Could you benefit from the wisdom of a Christian counselor?

5. Read Romans 5:3-5. What does this verse say about the role suffering plays in developing our character? And what is the result when the process is fully realized?

6. Have you ever tried to "use" God, and manipulate and control your life? What happened?

CHAPTER 8

1. Have you ever thought that obeying God's will meant you would be safe?

2. Did something happen to challenge that belief?

3. If so, in what ways did that affect your faith?

CHAPTER 9

1. Have you ever felt like you were following a "Bible-told-me-so Jesus," and a "somebody-told-me-so God"?

2. If so, what effect did that have on your faith?

3. Have you found a way to experience God for yourself? If so, how?

4. Erica shared some of her least favorite platitudes in Chapter 9. What are some Christian platitudes that you have found to be unhelpful or untrue in your faith journey? Why do you think Christians are compelled to say them?

5. "God was inviting me to slow down, to live in the pain and learn the lessons that only deep hurt and helplessness can teach: absolute trust and sweet dependence." Why do you think pain and helplessness are such effective teachers?

CHAPTER 10

1. Have you ever faced a situation that was completely and utterly out of your control? What was it?
2. How did that make you feel?
3. Was your first reaction to trust God and turn to him, or to try and fix it yourself?

CHAPTER 11

1. In the opening line, Erica says, "Questions were part of my ruining and my restoration." Have you ever noticed irony at play in the way God works in your life? Share an example.
2. What did you think when God revealed that he saw no difference between her spiritual condition and the woman on the street corner? Why do you think that was so disturbing to her?
3. Have you ever had God reveal your true nature? Was the revelation shocking? How did you respond?

4. Do you ever read the Bible and not really take the time to understand what it's saying? What's one thing you can do today to try and slow down and process what you read?

5. Discuss this quote by Madeline L'Engle: "The unending paradox is that we do learn through pain...I look back at my mother's life and I see suffering deepening and strengthening it. In some people I have also seem it destroy. Pain is not always creative; received wrongly, it can lead to alcoholism and madness and suicide. Nevertheless, without it we do not grow. (*Walking on Water*)

6. Erica listed two subtle things she learned about doubt as a child:

   1. To doubt meant you weren't a follower of Jesus.
   2. Looking for answers about faith in books besides the Bible was not good.

Share your thoughts about these beliefs. Why do you think those ideas were so damaging? Can you relate?

CHAPTER 12

1. Have you ever had a friend be there for you in the "ugly everyday"?
2. What did that look like for you? What did they do?
3. Is there someone in your life right now that could use that kind of friendship? How can you be an "ugly everyday" friend to them?

CHAPTER 13

1. Why do you think it's so important not to isolate yourself when you're struggling with your faith?
2. What are some fears that hold you back from being vulnerable with others?
3. Do you think the benefits of being open and vulnerable outweigh the risks? Why or why not?
4. Name something specific that good friends can teach us about being a good friend.

CHAPTER 14

1. Read Isaiah 54. What did the connection between the broken down palace and the words God spoke to Erica through that passage make you feel?
2. Have you ever felt like that broken down, crumbling palace?
3. If so, what emotions do the words of Isaiah 54 stir in you?

CHAPTER 15

1. Erica talked about the metaphorical way the bitter gourd represented her experiences in India. Do you have your own bitter gourd experience? How can you figure out a way to season and prepare it so you can receive its benefits?
2. Erica came to the conclusion that she may never know the answer to the "caused it or used it" question, and she was okay with that. How does it make you feel?
3. Even though we may never get the answers to all of our questions, do you still feel they're worth asking? Why or why not?

4. What role does time and perspective play in interpreting our experiences and examining our doubts?

5. Erica said, "God's wide-open mercy grants us the gift of choice, to see the good or not, to choose light over dark, to move toward God or away from him, but that same freedom also allows the pain in." What do you think that means?

6. What do you think the title—*Holy Doubt*—means?

7. Can you see God at work in your circumstances today? If not, does *Holy Doubt* leave you with hope that you will someday?

CHAPTER 16

1. What comes to mind when you think of the mystery of God?

2. Do you find God's mysterious nature comforting or frightening? Or both?

3. Which part of God's paradoxical nature do you find most comforting? Most disturbing?

4. Why do you think it's important for us to get comfortable with the mystery of God?

5. Why do you think it's dangerous for us to get too focused on one aspect of God's nature?

CHAPTER 17

1. Erica asked, "What if God is better than we ever dreamed or thought possible?" What ideas and thoughts does this stir in you? What are the implications for your situation?

2. Why do you think it's so important for us to learn to trust God?
3. Would you have a hard time praying the prayer that Francis Chan prayed? Why or why not?
4. What aspect of God's character makes you believe most in his trustworthiness?

Notes

Introduction
1. L'Engle, Madeline. (2001). *Walking on Water*. Colorado Springs: WaterBrook.

Chapter 4
1. Thompson, F. The Hound of Heaven. In Nicholson & Lee (Eds.), *The Oxford Book of English Mystical Verse* (239). (1917).

Chapter 5
1. Yancey, Philip. (1988). *Disappointment with God*. Grand Rapids: Zondervan.
2. Miller, Donald. StoryBrand podcast.

Chapter 7
1. Stanley, Andy. (2012). *Deep and Wide*. Grand Rapids: Zondervan.

Chapter 9
1. Stanley, Andy. (2016). Gods of the No Testament. Retrieved from http://northpoint.org/messages/who-needs-god/gods-of-the-no-testament/

Chapter 11

1. Lewis, C.S. (2009). *The Problem of Pain*. New York: HarperCollins ebooks
2. Yancey, Philip. (1988). *Disappointment with God*. Grand Rapids: Zondervan.
3. L'Engle, Madeline. (2001). *Walking on Water*. Colorado Springs: WaterBrook.

Chapter 13
1. Brown, Brené. (2018). *Dare to Lead*. New York: Random House.

Chapter 15
1. Stanley, Andy. (2012). *Deep and Wide*. Grand Rapids: Zondervan.

Chapter 16
1. Clegg, Tom. (2019). The Lord's Prayer—Thy Kingdom Come. Retrieved from https://bit.ly/2EHC0NT
2. Peterson, Eugene. (2018). Every Step an Arrival. New York: WaterBrook.

Chapter 17
1. Chan, Francis. *James*. RightNow Media. Accessed 2/13/19.
2. TerKeurst, Lysa. (2018). *It's Not Supposed to be This Way*. Nashville: Thomas Nelson.
3. Bevere, John and Lisa. (2017). "Conversations with John and Lisa Bevere."
4. Groeschel, Craig. (2018). *Hope in the Dark*. Grand Rapids: Zondervan.
5. Bevere, John. (2019). *God Where Are You?* Palmer Lake:Messenger.

6. Nieuwhof, Carey. (2018). *Didn't See it Coming*. New York: WaterBrook.

LET'S BE FRIENDS!

You can get connected, find out about upcoming books, and catch the latest blog posts from Erica at www.ericabarthalow.com.

Thank you so much for reading! I hope *Holy Doubt* has helped you feel less alone on the dark road through doubt and has shed a little light on your path. Please take a minute to head over to Amazon or Goodreads and leave a review.

Made in the USA
Columbia, SC
23 November 2019

83738335R00117